The Church Trap

ALSO BY ARTHUR HERZOG:

The War-Peace Establishment

The Church Trap

Arthur Herzog

THE MACMILLAN COMPANY

New York

The Macmillan Company, New York
Collier-Macmillan Canada Ltd., Toronto, Ontario
Printed in the United States of America

Contents

1452101

Introduction

This is not a book about theology, but rather about churches, about the religious style, about the American character expressing itself through organized religion. If, as some say, we are in the process of redefining ourselves as a nation, the religious identity will have to be redefined as well.

The "model," as the social scientists say, used here is the Protestant church. One reason is that the Protestants, typically rational and scientific in their approach, have given a good deal of thought and research to the central religious dilemma in America, how to survive without changing, or if fundamental changes are made, how to survive. Catholics and Jews confront similar problems but they can be seen somewhat more clearly through the Protestant focus. Then, though the WASP seems to have lost some of his confidence, the dominant style in America is still white Protestant—as Will Herberg puts it, in *Protestant Catholic Jew*, "The Anglo-Saxon type remains the American ideal to which all other elements are transmuted in order to become American"— which the other religions are forced to copy to some extent, at least. But I trust there are enough facts and illustrations to show that what applies to one branch of American religion generally applies to all.

At least some of the conclusions reached will not make church people particularly happy, but I have tried to be objective, even at the risk of sounding pessimistic and downbeat. If, as I think, the mental set of America at the present time is not well-suited to facing realistically either our international or domestic troubles, then religious particularism and Christian optimism must bear some of the responsibility. It's clear that massive adjustments must be made, and they will involve heavily the future of organized religion.

My many thanks to the ecclesiastical leaders, ministers, priests, nuns, rabbis, religious scholars and ordinary churchgoers whom I interviewed for this book; Prof. George LaNoue and Revs. George Webber and Samuel Southard for helpful comments on the manuscript; to the Misses Debra Kram, Nancy Bancroft and Mary Moss, and Mrs. Nancy Henderson, who assisted in the preparation; and to my wife, Lael Scott, just for being herself.

A. H.

East Hampton, New York
September, 1967

Chapter One

The Church Trap

WHAT on earth is happening out there, in those 320,000 churches across the land? Instead of rejoicing at the altars of the richest, most powerful religious organizations in history, they come to a funeral. Hurry! Change the neon from

J
SAVES
S
U
S

to

G
O
D

GOD IS DEAD

D
E
A
D

"All the Church is in ferment," said Pope Paul VI, who might have been speaking for any major American denomination or creed. But there is no agreement on the nature of the brew. Some people declare that the churches are poised on the brink of a New Reformation, even in a world which has been called post-Christian, post-ideological, post-just-about-everything. Others think the churches will muddle through; but within the churches themselves today also flourish small, highly vocal bands of latter-day Jeremiahs who predict for organized religion that ultimate of tragedies, decay and death with no hope for an after-life.

The debate is strange, for on paper at least, the churches appear to be marching confidently toward the third millennium. The familiar statistics have often been held up to the world as talismans of American rectitude. Two out of three Americans claim church membership, and 44 per cent of the population is said to comply with the promptings of the public service ads to "worship at the church of your choice" by showing up there once a week (a figure which must be viewed with skepticism, since some religious leaders do not believe the churches can hold that many people on Sundays, sitting or standing). "We are a religious people whose institutions presuppose a divine being," wrote Supreme Court Justice William O. Douglas, and so, in theory at least, religion, if not established, is sanctified by the state and is to be found on our coins, in our oaths, on cornerstones, in short almost everywhere. Evidently, too, Americans like the idea of big, strong churches, seeing them as an anchor against too much and too rapid change, a deterrent to crime in the streets, emblems of our souls. So the conventional portrait is that of a churchy America, as the Protestant theologian Gibson Winter puts it, "pious, pure, holy and noble in a wicked world."

Nonetheless, for organized religion in America not all the News is Good. Religious leaders today can be thought of increasingly as ecclesiastical executives who, in spreading the Lord's word, use computers and PERT (Program Evaluation Review Technique) and flow charts and talk about inputs, outputs and cost-effectiveness. (". . . the almost frantic propagation of modern methods," thought the famous German Protestant, Dietrich Bonhoeffer, who looked with alarm at the American religious scene, "betrays the dwindling of content.") The churches do not pay cash dividends but they are clearly interested in the management techniques of modern corporations. The Roman Catholic Church employs management consultants, and a leading Protestant denomination plans to hire a long-range planner who, "hopefully," would be a Christian, while a Southern Protestant denomination employed a Jew to make a study of its membership because it wanted objective answers. The information arriving at the major religious administration centers—like the National Conference of Catholic Bishops, in Washington, D.C., or the limited partnership of thirty-four Protestant denominations known as the National Council of the Churches of Christ in the U.S.A., in New York City, which occupies a large, glittering structure irreverently called by its occupants "the Godbox"—indicates that serious trouble may lie ahead.

Within church circles religious statistics are well-known for their inaccuracy, but some credence, it's thought, can be given to trends. The famous "religious revival" of the 1950's—to which the churches attached great hopes, and which prompted serious scholars to predict a genuinely religious America—now appears to have ended before the decade was out; ended, in fact, just as it was receiving maximum publicity. Since then the trends seem to be running against the churches, and for this reason, perhaps, the yearly releases on church membership are no longer headline news. Membership has been leveling off until it has fallen behind the growth of the general population. In 1965 church membership increased 1.3 per cent while the population rose 1.5 per cent. The Jews considered themselves lucky to hold their own against death, and the "bluechip" Protestant denominations, studying the figures, have begun to wonder if the WASP has lost his sting. "There is," says R. H. Edwin Espy, General Secretary of the National Council of Churches, "the probability of membership leveling off. There is an identifiable trend. It is a critical issue."

"We feel the tide started to flow out in 1958," says John F. Anderson, Executive Secretary of the Board of National Ministries of the Presbyterian Church in the U.S. The denomination has its roots in the South, where the churches are stronger than anywhere else in the country. Evidently the figures were engraved in his mind, for Anderson, a big man in two-toned shoes, was able to rattle off from memory, without hesitation, the statistical course of his million-member denomination. In 1958 the U.S. Presbyterians could show a net increase in membership of 20,000, which went down to 13,000 in 1960; 7,000 in 1964; 4,000 by 1965. In 1966 the increase was up to 5,000, hardly enough for a denominational sigh of relief.

This "decrease in the rate of increase," as it's called, has lasted long enough to be established as an ecclesiastical fact of life. It appears to be affecting almost all churches, regardless of race, color or creed. The possible exceptions to the rule are fundamentalist churches which still claim to be growing faster than the general population, and indeed, there might be solid reasons for thinking that conservative religions will grow for the precise reasons that liberal churches will shrink—the former appealing to both the traditionally minded and those afraid of change; the latter, in tailoring themselves to secular society, gradually losing their separate identity and reason for being. Just the same, the less ebullient Northern churchmen don't believe the fundamentalists apply the same rigor to statistics as evangelism. To them, Southern Baptist figures, for instance, are loaded with non-members, and it's true, according to one study, that in several largely Southern Baptist counties in Mississippi the reported church membership actually managed to exceed the *total* number of people who lived there.

But it's not simply membership that has the churches concerned. The Roman Catholic magazine *Commonweal*, pointing out that the church in 1967 had fewer educational institutions, parish elementary pupils, converts, nuns, seminarians, infant baptisms (down 84,096, for Catholics a significant statistic) and a very slow growth rate, went on to say, "U.S. Catholics are deep in their reassessment of traditional Catholicism. The Church has only begun to glimpse the consequences." One might expect to find the

Protestants of the future in Sunday School, and yet Protestant figures show sharp declines in Sunday School attendance, to the point where some churchmen would like to write off Sunday School altogether. College church programs attract only a miniscule proportion of students, and while once everybody could be depended on to tell the pollsters dutifully that he believed in God, a large and growing number of high school and college students describe themselves with the dread word "agnostic" or even "atheist." The disenchantment is evident even among Catholics, despite their emphasis on the centrality of the church and its teachings. Catholic leaders are said to be seriously worried by polls like one at a Jesuit high school showing that 84 per cent of the students disagreed with the church's position on birth control, 39 per cent did not pray and 45 per cent did not believe in churches.

On the one hand, then, the churches have fewer replacements in sight, while on the other the present church membership contains a high concentration of old people. This realization has led many churchmen to expect that before very long the decrease in the rate of increase will turn into an absolute decline, bottoming no one knows where. "At meetings of ministers in New York," says a well-informed Lutheran pastor, "there is the unspoken fear that the parishes are going under. One minister vies with the next for members. The result is deep suspicion." "It wouldn't surprise me if, by the year 2000, this parish is down to five per cent of its present membership," I was told by a gloomy young Episcopal clergyman in the West. "The Episcopal church will shrink and shrink. The church is like a fat woman, with too much water in the tissues."

So far the seepage has been slow, almost imperceptible, and one might think the elimination of excess fluid would be healthy. But the churches are committed to gaining adherents, not losing them, and for institutional as well as evangelical reasons. The twin breasts of American religion are membership and money, and if one sags so does the other. For a decade or more the churches have been embarked on an ambitious, billion-dollar-a-year building crusade. They now have an enormous physical plant to maintain and hopefully fill with parishioners on Sundays. There are steeples to paint, electric organs to repair, ministers to feed.

A religion, says Milton Steinberg, consists of four inseparable parts. It must have a philosophy of reality, a moral system, a regimen of rituals, individual and collective, and finally institutions that house, perpetuate and advance the other elements. The institutional church side of religion must not be overlooked, as it is by people who claim that democracy or communism are religions. And the institution—apart from its strictly doctrinal ideas —may have needs of its own, even though they are justified under some heading like "carrying on the Lord's work." Were you, say, a high church leader surveying the religious scene, observing a whittling away of your membership, a loss of your power to influence people, and a goodly amount of discontent and leaving among your clergy and intellectuals, you would be bound to think that something was wrong. You might well decide that religion should be more attractive, exciting, meaningful to peoples' lives— in a word, "relevant." You would be perfectly honest in feeling this, but at your back would be the needs, the institutional imperatives, of the church organization.

In fact, relevance—meaning not only such things as masses in English but a churchly participation in large public issues like peace, civil rights and poverty—is the battle cry of the churches today, except for the extremely conservative denominations. But relevance takes money and this is one substance the churchgoers have proved reluctant to give for the purposes of social action. Not only is the contribution of the average churchgoer less, in terms of his income and the value of the dollar, than it was thirty years ago, but almost all of what he does give is retained by the local parishes, in the building fund or for a new Hammond organ or electronic chimes. When a denomination must cut back on its social programs, as the United Presbyterian Church in the U.S.A. has warned its flock it would have to do unless greater generosity was forthcoming, the implications, for the theologians of relevance, are serious.

The specter that haunts an increasing number of ecclesiasts is the realization that, faced with penurious parishioners on the one hand and a strong desire to prove themselves relevant on the other, the churches can only make their brave march into the world with government funds. And this on top of what is potentially the most explosive issue confronting religion today—the surprising extent to which churches, parishes, ministers, colleges, hospitals and almost all the charities on which religion prides itself for "good works," are already heavily underwritten or subsidized by the state, meaning church-members and non-church-members alike.

Religion in America is caught in a sociological trap. One jaw represents the fixed expectations of the parishioners who want a solid church organization with all the trimmings, church-as-usual on Sundays, the same old rules by which they've always lived. "I've had ten children," an angry woman told her priest. "If they change the rules on birth control I'm quitting the church." The other jaw is the pressure of a society whose slackening interest in religion brings great pressure on the churches to modernize, to arouse public interest, to get "where the action is," to be vital, to prove that they do have a useful and honest social function. To change in this direction risks alienating the great bulk of church members, while not to change risks becoming ever more isolated from the secular society. Leadership and laity, then, have different ideas about church. The leaders want a platform, a place from which to be heard on social issues. It may well be that the churchly stress on the woes of secular society betrays an inability to talk to their own members in terms meaningful to them. For the laity does not appear to be deeply involved in the pronouncements and judgments the leadership makes to the world. Church members in America look to religion for guidance, support, direction, and help in personal problems, but to individuals churches have less and less to say.

The man in the middle, a principal victim of the church trap, religion's unlucky Pierre, is the minister. As a profession the clergy is at a gravely low ebb. Protestant seminaries report trouble attracting candidates, and those they do get are likely to be at the bottom of the academic pile. A leading Catholic educator, Kenneth M. Reed, S.V.D., calls the decline in Catholic seminarians a "cliff-drop," and, he says, "It is going to continue down and stay down for a long time." Fewer candidates plus more dropouts add up to a decimated clergy. "For us, the problems of the 1970's won't merely be staffing schools and hospitals," says a leading priest-psychologist, "but in finding priests to run the parishes." As it is, even with the free labor of priests and nuns, Catholic schools and hospitals are imploring more and more government support. If the Catholics, with only one priest per eight hundred churchgoers in the U.S., redouble their "prayers for more priests"—it may be an indication of how serious and worldwide a Catholic difficulty this is that the Diocese of Rome, heartland of Catholicism, is presently producing between one and five vocations *per year*—and wonder where the next generation's clergymen are coming from, so must the Jews wonder, with only about a hundred rabbis annually graduating in the U.S., and the Protestants, whose personnel problems are intensified by the desire of new ministers to serve in education, the "inner city," the poverty program, the church bureaucracy, anywhere but in the local parishes.

Word may have filtered down to them that all is not well with the parish minister. "I think between ten and twenty per cent of our clergy would quit tomorrow if they had a job option," I was told by a ranking Episcopal bureaucrat, "and many others are dissatisfied." A Presbyterian official, Rev. Edward S. Golden, a sort of minister to ministers, believes that at least 20 per cent of Presbyterian clergymen *ought* to quit. "Many ministers," he says, "when they face the reality of church life, rankle at it and may lose their faith, although they go on mechanically, that is as part of the church machine."

In the halcyon days of Protestantism sons of ministers often emulated their fathers and became ministers themselves, but this is less and less the case. "You were the first minister in our family and you will be the last," the son of a successful suburban minister in Detroit told his father. The son had watched his father perform, year after year, a delicate balancing act between what the minister thought was right and what his parishioners expected of him. It is no accident that most Protestant faiths today have begun to provide psychological services for disturbed ministers, where they can discuss their troubles and try to sort out their lives. In the opinion of those who provide psychological counsel for the clergy the pulpit today is an anxious seat, a place where potential neuroses are brought out in the open. And it is a sad commentary on the rigidity of American Protestantism that troubled ministers are often reluctant to look for help, because a minister, both by popular expectation and his own, isn't supposed to be *sick*, because of his connection with the divine.

The new openness of the Catholic Church has not extended to revealing the number of "fallen priests," but those close to the problem agree on its scope. "We sense," says Msgr. George Higgins, "that priests and nuns don't leave for the reasons they always did—authority and sex. There is something new in the air. I would call it a problem in Catholic identity." An abbot refers to the "mass exodus from the religious life," and nuns appear to be defecting in striking numbers—dropouts of 30 or 40 per cent in some orders seem to be occurring. Estimates on the number of fallen priests begin at five thousand and go on up—as compared to a priestly population of sixty thousand—but round numbers are only part of the problem. Also important is the shock to the Catholic nervous system—reflected in the interest displayed by the public in the fallen priests themselves, and in the rumors about defections flooding the priestly grapevines—that priests would actually choose to depart the sacred and high terrain of the church. The defectors, moreover, invariably say that they intend to remain Catholic, and to some Catholic authorities the real danger is that ex-priests, loosely banded together, will form a sort of anti-party within the church, undermining official authority and further confusing an already confused laity.

The Roman Catholic problem is always presented as unique, related to the great internal stresses that have wracked the church since the Second Vatican Council. And yet is Vatican II entirely the cause? Not according to John Cogley, former religion editor of *The New York Times* and now a resident intellect at the Center for the Study of Democratic Institutions at Santa Barbara. "The Council cannot be blamed for all this unrest. . . . The hour for revolutionary change had struck. . . . In other words, with or without the Council, we would have had the present headlines," Cogley, a Catholic himself, told a group of Catholic educators. He went on to predict, "Without rapid and drastic change there is, I think, little hope for the Church."

One finds gloomily parallel prophecies from the other faiths, from Jews who ask if anything will survive of Judaism but Jewish jokes and chicken soup, from Protestants who contributed to an angry symposium entitled *Who's Killing the Church?* (The churches are, they cry.) The church, declares an Episcopal minister named Malcolm Boyd, who tried to show precisely how hip and relevant a preacher can be by performing at a San Francisco nightclub, "is to be found somewhere in the position of the *Titanic* heading toward an iceberg."

Such judgments can be heard from high in the church structures, off-the-record or conveyed elliptically, but occasionally stated in black and white. "I always tell young ministers," explains an outspoken Episcopal bishop, Daniel Corrigan, "that before they get to the end of the road, this new church, that new rectory just won't be there. But if they know this ahead of time, if they know that other Christians without big, rich churches have lived effectively, they'll be all right." "We're in the rapids right now," says J. L. Sullivan, Executive Secretary of the powerful Southern Baptist Sunday School Board. "Some are upset by the turbulence and lose their sense of direction." "I compare the Church to a pilot running out of gas over the ocean," says John Wright, Bishop of Pittsburgh, a highly influential Catholic. "Either he slows down in the hope of conserving his fuel or speeds up in hope of getting there before it runs out. Both ways, the hope is probably in vain."

Usually each faith is treated parochially, examined under its own lights, so that Catholics are said to stumble over sex, freedom and authority, Protestants over the Death of God and accusations that they are "weak, tardy, equivocal and irrelevant," Jews over the issue of separatism and the survival of Jewish culture. But though we try to individuate the faiths, it appears that each is undergoing a similar crisis, that the malaise of one is common to all, and that such distinctions in symptomatology as do appear on the surface are really gauges of how far the illness has progressed.

The church crisis is deeply bound up with the myths and aspirations of those who make up the bulk of church membership in America, the white middle class, with its position in the country and the world, with its philosophy, and with its perception of the sacred, meaning reality and power which it wants to locate as close as possible to itself, to its communities and to its country. As Mircea Eliade points out, the feeling of I-am-at-the-center is integral to primitive religion and there is every reason to think it is carried over in church organizations today. But if such beliefs were insecurely held, if the person, community or country had begun to doubt that it was indeed at the center, if it had begun to question its own myths and aspirations, a certain confusion in identity would have to result. In fact, religion in America displays the symptoms of a serious crisis in identity, and it is not too much to say that the churches, though still possessed of large resources and reservoirs of good will, are at the moment holding operations, searching for something to do, something for which to live, some clearer conception of just why they are here and what they are here *for*.

The term "identity crisis" came into common coinage as a result of *Young Man Luther*, a book by Erik H. Erickson, a psychoanalyst, who defined his conception as "the major crisis of adolescence [which] occurs in that period of the life cycle when each youth must forge for himself some central perspective and direction, some working unity, out of the effective remnants of his childhood and the hope of his anticipated adulthood; he must detect some meaningful resemblance between what he has come to see in himself and what sharpened awareness tells him others judge and expect him to be."

The notion of an identity crisis aptly describes the condition of organized religion today. There is the same probing at the deepest level with questions about self-worth and self-value. There is the same struggle to forge some "central perspective and direction, some working unity," the same effort "to detect a meaningful resemblance" between the teachings of the faiths and the realities of church life. "Erickson believes," writes Harvey Cox in *The Secular City Debate*, "that the key to a successful negotiation of an identity crisis is the individual's creative reappropriation of his previous identities into a new one which stands in continuity with the past but is now freed to deal with the future." But there is no guarantee that the religious identity crisis *can* be resolved in this or any other way.

Religion has been defined by Knight Dunlap as "the institution or feature of culture which takes, in the service of mankind, those functions for which there is no other institution or for the undertaking of which no other institution is as yet adequately prepared." Religion, in other words, has, or ought to have, functions in society, things it does that command allegiance, respect and support. A leading sociologist of religion, Prof. Thomas F. O'Dea, gives two such functions: "One is a larger view of the beyond, in the context of which deprivation and frustration can be experienced as meaningful. The other is the ritual means for facilitating a relationship to the beyond which gives enough security and assurance to human beings to sustain their morale."[1]

Specifically, O'Dea goes on, religion "identifies the individual with his group, supports him in uncertainty, consoles him in disappointment, attaches him to society's goals, enhances his morale,

[1] Thomas F. O'Dea, *The Sociology of Religion* (Englewood Cliffs, N.J.: Prentice-Hall Inc., 1966), pp. 14-16.

and provides him with elements of identity. It acts to reinforce the unity and stability of society by supporting social control, enhancing established values and goals, and providing the means for overcoming guilt and alienation. It may also perform a prophetic role and prove itself an unsettling or even subversive influence in any particular society."

Identification, consolation, support, morale-building, even subversion—there is nothing here uniquely provided by religion. Identification? It's true, of course, that almost everybody labels himself Catholic, Jew or Protestant. These were once important "badges of belonging," as Max Lerner calls them, in a society that was prejudiced against immigrants who were forced to huddle in national-religious congregations. Habit still operates, and when a person puts "P," "C," or "J" on his hospital registration card, after "Religion, if any," he may well be referring to his ethnic heritage. Then, though this is slowly changing, the social and legal customs of the country still force a religious identification on people, for instance in adoption proceedings, where by law children must be placed in homes of a similar religious background, or immigration procedure where churches have been tacitly allowed to select the candidates,[2] or merely in the forms, where it is somehow easier, more acceptable and less dangerous to put "Protestant," "Catholic," or "Jew" than "atheist," "agnostic," "no religion," or even "secularist." (It is difficult to imagine what the average clerk would do with *that* word.) It seems entirely fair to say that, in being supplied with and using ready-made identification-labels of the Protestant-Catholic-Jew trinity, people have foregone the opportunity to find meaningful identifications for themselves, if indeed such are required. And the ones given them by religion are not always convincing. "The Jew still asks: 'What am I?'" writes Rabbi Morris Adler. "And perhaps in the process he has provided the best possible answer at present: A Jew is a person who is always asking, 'What am I?' Certainly this definition is as authentic and comprehensive as any other."

[2] See Chapter Seven.

Ease death? A study of dying patients at a Chicago hospital indicates that non-believers died as gracefully as believers. The group that died badly were people, believers and non-believers, who had not come to terms with themselves. A great many religious bad-diers, the researchers (including a chaplain) decided, were pseudo-religious and did not really believe the axioms of their own faith, and that atheists and agnostics could die just as peacefully as believers would indicate that religion can lay no special claims to personal succor. The adage, "There are no atheists in foxholes," runs counter to the experience of every G.I. who has seen military action.

Small wonder then that the churches worry about "secular alternatives to religion." And the list of provinces religion has already abandoned is impressive. The churches have foregone the claim to religious unification, to overt (though not covert) tax support, or to the control of the public educational process. "Expansion of modern government has radically diminished the dependence of the average citizen on churches as the source of education and health care," says one of the leading students of church-state relations, Dr. George LaNoue. The churches no longer reserve the right to draw the guidelines for culture and philosophy. The Sunday Schools, where the churches indoctrinate the young, are in deep trouble and may well be abandoned. The churches' hold over laws governing divorce, birth control and abortion is weakening, and except for dwindling enclaves of the faithful, the churches no longer set the rules for family life and sex. One could look far to find a comment on the state of religion as penetrating as a report of the liberal Catholic journal, Commonweal, on a recent conference on Church and the Family: "The drafting of practical recommendations was hobbled by the delegates' prevailing reluctance and in some cases confessed inability to propose standards of sexual morality either for Christians or for secular man."

"Founded by Jesus Christ, A.D. 33," asserts an early 1900's legend on a church wall in Nashville, Tennessee, and from this simple faith and rocklike certainty one spans half a century to arrive at "WORSHIP GOD IN YOUR CAR, Casually Dressed, Comfortably Seated—Valley Forge Drive-In Theater" (which probably also showed *The Bible* and charged admission). Over this space of time, as the sociologist Daniel Bell puts it, "The old primary group ties of family and local community have been shattered; ancient parochial faiths are questioned; few unifying standards have taken their place." An oleagenous glow may continue to illuminate the altarpieces, but for practical wisdom people look elsewhere, to scientists, psychiatrists, those with professional credentials. Contrary to the hopeful predictions of religious scholars, there is no sign that any large number of secular intellectuals have become "fellow-travelers of faith." It is not because the churches, eternally optimistic that everyone will come to see the light, haven't tried. The United Presbyterian Church in the U.S.A., for instance, started an experimental ministry at Cape Kennedy, with the idea of lending its spiritual insights to the scientists in the space program, but the scientists apparently felt they could aim for the stars—or Peking—without the aid of organized religion. The secular intellectuals not only determine public policy but they give legitimacy to it, replacing the clergy as standard-setters. The churches, denominational leaders and preachers, take positions on war, nuclear weapons, race and the like—indeed, they are *expected* to—but their predictable pronunciamentos on public matters are conveniently ignored, not just by the men in power but by their own constituents. On one issue where organized religion spoke with considerable unity—against the war in Vietnam— there is no indication that churchly protests had any effect on public policy.

A reason the churches are ignored is that, like ladies of high virtue, they can be counted upon to say, "No." "Thou shalt *not*," thunder the churches—make war, fornicate, covet, commit adultery, or as in the actual case of an order of cloistered nuns, die without the Mother Superior's permission. My own memory of church consists mostly of a pink-cheeked gentleman shaking a verbal finger, and what positives he accentuated sounded suspiciously like platitudes even to young ears. The churchly identity thus fostered is almost entirely negative. The Catholic theologian, Gabriel Moran, speaks of the "negations inherent to Protestantism and incorporated into Catholicism. By seeing God's function as the forgiver of sin, by exalting faith at the expense of reason, post-Reformation Christianity could not find God by going beyond man because it could not accept man." The churches have not only defined man in their own terms, but they have rigidly clung to their definitions even when man, as the new society of abundance has made possible, has insisted on defining himself in new ways. By remaining essentially nay-sayers and conservers—in matters, say, of sex—the churches have paid an enormous price in believability.

All might be well for the churches had they been able to stay with religion as expressed in the local parishes, but change has been pressing hard. Half the population moves every five years and the migration from town to city has hacked away at religion's rural roots. Vice-President Hubert Humphrey once predicted that within not too many years rural America, from the Appalachians to the Rockies, would be virtually deserted except for the cities, occupied only by a few farmers and caretakers. In this atmosphere of dislocation the churches' private vision of the ideal society is still that of a rural communality, in which services are arranged so as not to interfere with milking time and where people had common backgrounds and interests.

"Churches are by definition communal," says the sociologist Norman Birnbaum, "whereas society tends toward privatization. The churches assume there is a sort of unified public which wants guidance, when in fact there is none." The ladies' groups, the church suppers, the bazaars and prize cakes, the socials, the picnics, the inevitable photos of plain people in rimless spectacles singing—although the denominational magazines show that such events still comprise church life, they are clearly images of days past. The newer, more sophisticated parishes in the suburbs are under heavy fire from within the churches for being parochial, inward-looking, a mere social club, selfish and a spiritual luxury. "The attempt," says Gibson Winter, "to perpetuate the local parish or congregation as a basic unit of the Christian church is doomed to failure."

It's not at all surprising, in view of the circumstances in which organized religion finds itself, that the churches should long to attract new people, to appeal to the urbanites and the young, to reclaim their centrality and importance. So we find, presided over by slightly anxious but always smiling "get-with-it" ministers (crammed with Harvey Cox's guidebook to religious urbanity, *The Secular City*), the jazz vespers and beat services, the guitars, the lonely-hearts socials and showings of what looks to the more strait-laced like prurient art—to bring in the customers. But religion's modernity smacks of borrowed gear, as though change does not spring from genuine inner impulse but is imposed from the outside, by external necessity. Walter Kaufmann speaks of the churches' attempts "to balance the imposing archaism of most of their thought with some of the latest jargon," and indeed the churches want so hard to swing. They would like to be "relevant," "where the action is," "at the cutting edge," to "come alive in a church of dialogue" in the "inner city." The goal for themselves and for others is to become "truly human," to all but religious ears a tautology. Repeated endlessly by writer after writer in religious journals, catchwords like these reveal religion's inability to come up with fresh ideas of its own.

One of the brightest aspects of the current church scene is the sincere attempt by most branches of organized religion to take a forthright position on the issue of race. Here, as nowhere else, the churches have been able to exert some leverage, and there are countless examples of heroism among the clergy. And yet, even on the race question, there are signs that the churches are not precisely comfortable as crusaders. For the churches, not believing that civil rights activism was proper for them, were late in joining the fray. The Roman Catholic bishops did not take a stand until

1958, almost a hundred years after the Civil War, the Protestants not much earlier and in some cases later. Many of the famous priests and nuns who marched at Selma, Alabama, would not have gotten there if orders from a certain bishop rescinding permission had arrived on time. In many cities rabbis are still conspicuously absent from civil rights organizations, and the role of many clerics in the history of civil rights could easily be called "profiles in cowardice." Some churches today are badly divided on the race issue, with parishes withholding funds from denominations that move too far, too fast, and acting as a brake on the religious commitment. Particularly depressing for those who want religion to take a passionate stand on race is the fact that Negro clerics within the white denominations are leaving. For them, the churches' progress has been too slow, and the position of the Negro in a white church structure remains ambiguous.

There is, too, a larger issue here. For if, as Reinhold Niebuhr has said, "The race crisis saved the churches from irrelevance," then what can be thought of their relevance beyond it? If the Negro is Christ today, who will He be tomorrow? If the race issue is solved, what else will make religion relevant? Is it true, then, that Christianity has no intrinsic relevance? If as one Christian radical puts it, "Christian faith equals public involvement," then, strictly speaking, there can be no Christian faith outside of public involvement, and what can be said about the panoply of religious liturgies, prayers and services, of religious belief itself? For one can easily have public involvement without the Christian or any other faith, and if good deeds define the Christian then we have no need of churches to define Christians for us.

The evidence suggests that organized religion is moving on exceedingly treacherous waters and whether it can circumnavigate is by no means sure. Caught in a crisis of identity, lacking a clear relationship with society, confronting unrest in its clergy and declines in its growth, the church has three possible futures:

First, churches can respond actively to the gnawing discontent within the religious organizations and a growing disconcern without. To advocates of this way, it means violently wrenching the churches out of their old frames, committing them entirely to social action, progress and the realities of urban life. It means taking churchly eyes off otherworldly horizons and fastening them securely on this one. It means putting church money where its mouth is, and that implies an end to church building funds, probably the abandonment of the local parishes for a geographic, ecumenic, city-wide one. But this, the secularization of religion, carries grave risks. The doctrinal side of religion might hardly exist at all. Already the Episcopal Church has abandoned the notion of heresy, which would seem to indicate that there is little to be heretical about. If it comes to pass that the Pope is not infallible, even in matters of faith and morals, if bishops are elected by popular vote, if priests can marry and nuns serve only a few years before departing to raise families, how will one define the Roman Catholic Church? How will a Catholic be different from a Protestant? How will the Protestant Church, having jettisoned the supernatural, prayer, authority in moral matters, and so on, having committed itself to liberal social causes, differ, say, from Americans for Democratic Action? Why should the individual join one rather than the other? And what *would* a Jew be?

Such developments in the churches, moreover, would alienate the conservative parishioners who populate and largely finance the parishes, confuse the faithful and pious who find in religion a refuge from change, and risk a sharp decline in membership, a serious split between liberals and conservatives, or both. It is a possibility no red-blooded organization could lightly take, and those who threaten the church structure will almost surely be branded as enemies. Indeed, as Patrick Cardinal O'Boyle of Washington, D. C., has already said, "Today the enemies of religion, and of the Catholic Church in particular, are more likely to come from within."

The second possibility, equally repugnant to religion's organization men, is a conscious retreat from denominations back to sects. The sects might (though probably would not) teach a social gospel, but they certainly would put high-minded emphasis on religious doctrine, their separate identity, and would follow their own beliefs and practices, no matter how odd-ball they seem to the outside world. The general society would hear them in their own genuine and perhaps remote tongue (how significantly aloof and other-worldly the Papal language still sounds). But the sects could not have their holy wafers and eat them too. They would be forced to assent to the proposition that Protestants and Catholics, like Jews, are minority cultures in an irreligious state. Secular man would be recognized for what he is, the dominant social force, and the notion that our institutions are underwritten by an Almighty, in the sense that Fort Knox guarantees our currency, would be abandoned. The churches, standing on their own feet, would be taxed. The sects would have the virtue of being honest, to themselves and others, and on their own example, not overblown religious publicity or attempts to manipulate power, they would rest their case. At least the churches would have a chance to show the validity (or irrelevance) of the religious ideal, and the vague and unpleasant odor of spurious sanctity which still hangs over the United States would be dispelled.

Here, too, risks abound for religion, for the Jews, who have tried to preserve a sect-religion, also face absorption into the American blotter. But the third possibility, to hang, or try to hang, motionless in the tides of change, is the greatest risk. Changelessness, after all, is death.

Chapter Two

Dishonest to God?

At least until recently, when sagging growth has caused the churches earnest soul-searching, American Christianity has annually rejoiced three times—at Christmas, Easter, and when the denominations issue their reports on membership. By their own reckoning, anyway, there is still cause for churchly hosannas. In 1967, exactly 124,682,422 Americans—two-thirds of the population—were claimed as members of Protestant, Roman Catholic, Jewish, Eastern Orthodox and Buddhist bodies, while the rest of the people, almost to a man, identified themselves as Protestant, Catholic or Jew. The three religious communities are said to embrace almost the entire population, and if elections were held purely on religious lines in this country an atheist would get less than 5 per cent of the vote.

Such figures are treated with awe in Europe, where for some years now religion has been on the skids, while here they are treated with the authority of divine writ. Their sources are polls and surveys, but the bible of churchly calculations is the *Yearbook of American Churches*, published annually by the National Council of the Churches of Christ in the U.S.A. The *Yearbook*, although it hasn't always appeared under this name, has been in existence since 1916, and thus has acquired considerable familiarity with its own findings. In preface after preface, with Christian humility, the editors have warned that the figures are an "altogether elementary assembling of materials generally gathered by mail from officials of religious bodies," and, as they said in 1967, should be "used with care and interpreted judiciously." Such caveats have been ignored.

Religion and statistics, it might be thought, are at opposite ends of human concern, but in practice the churches have followed corporations in emphasizing fat figures and solid annual growth. (If religion were sold like stocks you would have the "high fliers" like the booming Southern Baptists and the Roman Catholics, the "blue chip" denominations—Episcopalians, Congregationalists and Presbyterians—and those with small growth potential like the Jews.) At least one would expect religion to observe a mathematical Golden Rule. For almost a quarter-century the *Yearbook* was under the editorship of the late Dr. Benson Y. Landis, one of the few men in America with a firm grip on what religious statistics mean, and don't. Shortly before his death I asked Dr. Landis if the figures were accurate.

"Not very," he said. "I'm not a statistician, you know, but an educator. I've never made any pretence that the religious statistics approached hard fact. At the beginning the aim wasn't to disseminate the figures—because they were rough estimates only—but to compile what we had. However, the public relations spirit has penetrated religion, and people here at the N.C.C. wanted to publish the figures on the theory that they would make news. They did, and now everybody uses them. Frankly, considering what the statistics represent, I pronounce myself surprised." The "Protestant Pentagon," the National Council of Churches, occupies a glossy building on Riverside Drive in New York City, and it's not necessary to look far for an example of a surprising religious statistic. Next door is the Riverside Church, administered by both the United Church of Christ and the American Baptists. The congregation is counted twice in the *Yearbook*, once by each denomination, and stands as a reminder that religious statistics must not be taken on faith. To a Doubting Thomas at the NCC, "The promotional element has swallowed up any kind of discipline."

It should be observed that no other source for overall U.S. religious statistics exists. The last American religious census was held in 1936, and ministers were compelled to answer questions about their churches on pain of fines and imprisonment if they refused. Even so, there was an organized protest, and when in 1957 a statistical sampling was tried once more by the Census Bureau the protests were such, especially from religious groups like the Jews who felt the separation of church and state was endangered, that the project was dropped. Similarly, plans to put religious questions in the 1970 census have been shelved. The *Yearbook* stands alone, then, its august figures unchallenged and unchecked.

The *Yearbook*'s figures are compiled from reports submitted by some two hundred and fifty religious bodies on such pertinent matters as membership, Sunday School attendance, and the numbers of clergymen. A few groups, like the Christian Scientists (Church of Christ, Scientist, which in 1936 had 268,915 adherents), refuse today to supply such information on doctrinal grounds, but the staggering spread of American religious expression is almost fully represented here. The Protestants, with 69,-088,183 members, come in first, as is natural in a Protestant land, but it crosses the mind that, considering the depth of Protestant differences, their denominations ought to be treated separately. In that case, the Roman Catholics, with 46,864,910 communicants, are in undisputed first place. Next come the Southern Baptists, who in recent years have overtaken the Methodists. Both have over 10,000,000 members, as compared to the Jews, with 5,600,000, who edge out the Presbyterians and Episcopalians. (The conventional ratio that has been worked out is 3-2-1—Protestant, Catholic, Jew. Free, though doubtless tax-deductible, radio and TV time is offered by the networks for "religious hours" on this basis. (It's symptomatic of the static that gets in American heads on religious matters that the Negroes are lumped in with the white Protestants and have little if any free network time.)

Although the larger groups account for most of the church membership they are far outnumbered as organizations by the smaller ones. There are twenty-one Eastern Churches alone, like the Greek Orthodox, with 1,735,000 members and the Holy Ukrainian Autocephalic Orthodox Church in Exile with 5,000. There are Buddhists and Christadelphians and evangelical groups like the Pillar of Fire or the Church of Daniel's Band (membership 200) down to the Church of Jesus Christ (Cutlerites—Latter Day Saints) with all of twenty-two members. The *Yearbook* is packed with echoes of political events, theological controversies, splits, mergers and the like, and it is perhaps more valuable as history or social commentary than as "statistics." Indeed, the great diversity may give a false impression of real strength.

It's none too difficult—as the *Yearbook*'s editors are the first to admit—to find cracks in the imposing columns of figures. One of the most damaging is that the numbers were gathered in widely varying points of time. The *Yearbook* statistics are *all* roundly out of date. Even the most recent returns in the so-called 1967 annual were supplied in 1966 by the denominations and represent tabulations for 1965 or 1964, but some of the tallies may be ten, twenty or even thirty years old for sects which have not seen fit to report since. The *Yearbook*, following its hands-off policy of letting denominations speak for themselves, feels it can do no more than print and reprint, edition after edition, the same bearded figures. Some religious groups—the five large Negro groups, for instance, or the white Southern ones—do not have anything like an accounting system and their numbers are little more than guesses. Considering organized religion's implacable urge to grow, it's unlikely that such guesses would err on the low side.

But it's not merely outdated and patchwork calculations that make the *Yearbook*'s widely bruited figure of 124,682,422 church members look doubtful. For evangelical, doctrinal and cultural reasons many religious groups hand in statistics which, by any standards but their own, would be called inflated. Such bodies have their own conceptions of membership and naturally defend them. Still, because the statistics are presented without qualifications, and then used breezily to prove what a churchgoing (and God-fearing) people Americans are, it seems only fair to inquire what the numbers mean.

Take, for instance, the "ethnic" religions like the Greek Orthodox or the Romanian Orthodox Episcopate of America. For such groups concepts of community and church are inseparable. All members of the ethnic or national group who can be identified are counted as *church* members, whether or not they have a *religious* affiliation. The same is true of the Jews who may be identified as Jewish by the appearance of a name on a list of donors to Jewish charities. Some say half, some say a good many less Jews are synagogue members or hold services at home.

Jewish logic is that, especially in the melting pot, it's vital to preserve the Judaic cultural-religious identity. "The Jewish religion," said Dr. Salo Baron, a leading contemporary Jewish historian, "has never been a religion in the Christian sense, primarily related to worship, prayer and theology. It was essentially a peculiar way of life. Even today the Jews who get together for social reasons, for charitable or defense purposes in a typical Jewish organization, are performing a Jewish religious service, although they do not quite know this is religion." Nor may they quite know they have become a statistic. The question of whether one should be allowed to become a number without one's consent has never been explored.

By strict definition, one is a Jew when one embraces the Jewish faith or is born from a Jewish mother. The question next arises as to how the Jews know that there are 5,600,000 people who fill the requirements. The answer is breathtakingly simple: They don't. The figure is described by such authorities as Dr. Nathan Goldberg, Professor of Sociology at Yeshiva University in New York City, as "pure guesswork." Some forty years ago there was a Jewish-run Jewish census, to whose results, assuming a growth in the Jewish population, the Jews have merely added from time to time, as seemed prudent. But not only was the original census highly questionable, so too is Jewish growth, at least since World War II. Canadian census figures show a very low Jewish birth rate, for example, and Russian-born Americans, who can be assumed to be largely Jewish, have among the lowest birth rate in the population. Such facts have led experts like Dr. Goldberg to conclude that there are fewer than 5,600,000 Jews in the U.S.[1]

Faced with the suspiciously round number of 5,600,000, the Jews have no other choice but to divide it up among the three main Jewish sects. The problem has been solved in the thoroughly practical fashion of religious people dealing with statistics. According to one Jewish authority, "The Reform Jews say what they think their membership is. The Conservatives announce theirs. The Orthodox Jews take all the rest."

Like Jewish ones, Catholic calculations are by no means as obvious as published figures suggest. Doctrinally, writes Michael E. Schlitz, "The Catholic is not in any relevant sense a member of the Catholic church 'of his own free will.' Once the individual accepts the community's invitation to Baptism . . . he accepts likewise the territorial structure of the parish. He cannot withdraw

[1] Not all Jews agree. Some think there are many more than 5,600,000 Jews, but they are not identified because they have dropped all religious affiliation. The evidence suggests this view is mistaken, and that, with Jewish intermarriage sharply increasing, the Jews will have increasingly grave trouble maintaining their present numbers, however many there are.

from the community because his membership in a particular parish is defined for him by his Baptism and his residential address." But this does not settle everything. To be included in the Catholic population you are supposed to have at least a nominal connection with the organized church or else, though still canonically Catholic, you are not counted in the statistics. The question is how well do Catholics subtract.

Catholic population figures are harvested by a New York firm named P. J. Kenedy & Sons, which publishes them annually in a weighty tome called *The Official Catholic Directory.* Perhaps the inclusion of "official" is meant to add authenticity, but Kenedy has no trained statisticians on its staff—indeed, it farms out the figures for collating. In any case the *Directory* is dealing with the rawest kind of data. Each year every parish submits a population report to the diocese, and the 153 dioceses and archdioceses submit a total to P. J. Kenedy. Just how the system works in practice was explained to me by Father Joseph Scheuer, co-author of *The De-Romanization of the American Catholic Church* and Professor of Sociology at Fordham University:

"At each parish unit the resident parson gets the questionnaire. He doesn't usually fill it out himself, but gives it to an assistant, who puts down his general impression of how many go to Mass. There isn't usually a head count. The tendency is to go back to the year before and up or down the number more or less by guesswork. The priest might want to minimize the figure because of the Cathedraticum, or the tax for the diocese, which a parish pays according to its membership. The figures then go to the diocese, which in some cases might change them, suspecting, for instance, that the priest wants a new school, or for its own reasons. They then go to P. J. Kenedy, which wants to square the total with Catholic population figures from last year, minus 'leakage' [the Catholic term for dropouts], plus converts, plus new baptisms, minus deaths. There is never a decrease or a modified rate of increase. It is always the total population of last year plus a prudent increase for this," according to Father Scheuer. There are informed Catholics who believe that a sort of statistical conspiracy exists to conceal the fact that there are many more Catholics than appear on the record books. This may well be true, under the loosest definition of a Catholic. The "base" from which priests decide whether membership is up or down—that is, the ultimate number of parishioners—is a census which parishes are supposed to run every five years as a matter of course, but which may take place every ten, fifteen or twenty years, if at all. Such censuses often report more Catholics in the parish than had been suspected but the questions do not get into church membership or the frequency of attendance. They want to know, "Are you a Catholic? Were your parents Catholic? Were you baptized Catholic?" The busy priest is left to discover how many Catholics in the parish are "lapsed" or "dormant" and should therefore be stricken from the record.[2]

A prominent Catholic bishop who refuses to be quoted adds the following: "There are all kinds of reasons for playing the numbers game. A priest might want to play up the number of his parishioners to show what a good job he is doing. But he might wish to play them down, on the grounds that if his parish is too big it will be divided. My feeling is that the pressures balance out, so that those reported do represent a fair reading of those who are part of the operative church. But this figure includes an enormous number of freeloaders who represent a great burden because they are noncontributors."

It seems obvious that a good many lapsed Catholics—estimated by the well-known Catholic sociologist, Father Joseph Fichter, at 30 per cent of the baptized—wind up in the church-member column. Many other Catholics whose connection with an organized church is very marginal—who may attend, as the saying goes, three times, at birth, marriage and funeral—may *think* of themselves as Catholic, and having said so, appear as another Catholic

---

[2] There must also be Catholic dogs—one New York kennel refused to sell an old English sheepdog to a Protestant family, saying puppies should go to homes of the same religion as the ones from which they came.

digit. The prevalence of such Catholics once led *Osservatore Romano*, the newspaper of the Vatican, to lament that only one-half of alleged Catholics in the world were really of the faith. Catholic figures, moreover, are swelled 25 per cent or more by the inclusion of children under thirteen. "If Protestant churches counted their adherents as generously as Catholic statisticians count theirs," wrote Paul Blanshard in *American Freedom and Catholic Power*, "it is likely that Protestants could claim almost three times as many adherents as the Catholic Church claims."

But this is manifestly unfair to the Catholics. For one thing, several Protestant churches also count baptized people, who may be children, in the total. The Moravians do, and the Episcopalians have two figures, one for baptized and one for communicants, meaning parishioners who have been confirmed. The communicant column is about one-third less than the baptized. The Lutherans actually keep three sets of numbers, one for baptized, one for people who have only the loosest church connections, and one for adult, confirmed, regular church attenders. Doctrine aside, the latter figure is a much better index of church members, but it is the larger figure which finds its way into the *Yearbook*. And even the denominations who say they only count adults may have singular definitions as to what an adult is. Baptists, for instance, are frequently baptized and become church members at the age of eight.

There is no reason to suspect, either, that WASPs keep better records than anyone else. "It is found," Dr. Landis once wrote, "that statistics of religious affiliation generally originate with the unstandardized records kept by clergymen or lay clerks in over three hundred thousand local churches, who are for the most part untrained." (The clergymen or lay clerks, that is.) Protestant bookkeeping was described some years ago as follows: "The turned-over corner of a card may distinguish the active from the inactive, and a blue pencil mark the resident from the non-resident. Someone in the church will have a list of Sunday-School pupils and this list may or may not show which of them are church members. Various membership lists will be found in the hands of their respective officers, but are seldom assembled in one list. The financial authorities of the church will have their subscription list and roll of other supporters. The regularity of attendance of individuals will rarely be recorded, and there will be little agreement as to what constitutes regularity . . ." In this respect the churches are unchanged.

Irregularities persist in church accounting which, in the computer age, would be tolerated nowhere else, and sometimes it seems that religious figurings have all the reality of the photographer's sign at a southern county fair: "Get your picture taken with the Holy Ghost." Ministers arriving at new pulpits have been shocked to learn that their members are also counted as members of other churches in the community. There are, writes Wilbur Zelensky, "undoubtedly numerous cases where a significant number of members are reported for counties in which they do not reside." An American Baptist parish turned out to have 800 instead of the 1,700 reported members who found their way into the *Yearbook*. A Southern Baptist minister in Dallas confided to an official of another denomination that out of 12,000 members he did not know where 3,000 of them were.

Let us dwell a moment with the Southern Baptists. They are an interesting case in point, because not only do they claim to be the fastest growing and largest Protestant denomination, and proud of it, but their theological conservatism does not interfere with an up-to-date attitude toward research and statistics. "Why, we spend eight hundred thousand dollars a yeah just on *postage*," says an official of the Sunday School Board in Nashville, Tennessee. Among the figures collected by Southern Baptist staticians is one not often noticed, that out of the ten-million-plus members of the denomination, some three million are listed as non-resident, meaning that they do not worship at the church which carries their name, and their whereabouts, much less their continued existence, is often unknown. "We assume that they go to church somewhere," says a Southern Baptist official, but this can only mean they are counted twice. The church has much of its strength in the rural South, and as the rural population declines, so naturally will church membership in the areas, but to have one's name removed from the rolls of a Southern Baptist church requires a letter of transfer from the congregation and such letters are often impossible to get. The situation that results is the one described earlier, where the church population exceeds the actual number of people living in some places. Churches, evidently, are far more zealous about counting people coming into the parishes than leaving them.

What is the reason for this numerolatry, the worship of numbers? One reason may be to impress politicians and others who might help—churches are not immune to the drive for institutional power, which can be reflected in size. Partly, too, the bigness urge is evangelical; that is, if you're interested in saving souls you want to save as many as you can. Church people like to think that there are millions of others who share their beliefs. "Our statistics," I was told by one religious leader, "are our way of being personal with our members, of dramatizing our faith."

Religion, anyone? Such is the urge of parishes for more members that some churches will do almost anything to attract them. Messiah Lutheran in Philadelphia, advertising that "Photos may be taken," recently used a live donkey in its Palm Sunday service. (One wonders if the altarboys had extra duties with a shovel.) The same church released, at Easter, "One thousand Resurrection helium balloons" containing "Christ Is Risen" cards. A similar device was tried not long ago by the Assembly of God Church in Frankfurt, Indiana, which placed inside its thousand balloons gift certificates ranging from fifty cents to fifty dollars. The certificates had to be presented at church school services at Easter to be redeemed, and one can be sure that *this* kind of redemption was accompanied by a membership pitch.

In the last few years some of the "blue chip" Protestant denominations, aware that when it comes to religious statistics things are not always as they seem, have begun to look at membership realistically. Parishes which have adopted serious accounting procedures have reported drops of 25 per cent or more. A spokesman for the United Church of Christ, the union of the Congregationalists and the Evangelical and Reformed Church, admits that probably only two-thirds of published membership is bona fide, the remainder being composed of inert people carried on church rolls. Within these denominations one finds even more pessimistic appraisals as to the actuality of membership figures compared to the published statistics. A high-ranking Episcopal Bishop, Daniel Corrigan, makes a practice when he enters a new town of counting the churches, estimating the number of seats and the number of services, and comparing them with the population figures. "Even assuming church services are all full, I would bet the reported church total is double the real one," Bishop Corrigan says.

But the churches are far from full. By definition a church is an inefficient institution, since its facilities for worship are used only a fraction of the time, but even on Sundays the pews are often empty. The Protestants, especially, suffer from what they have called "rampant overchurching" because every sect has to have its own place of worship, and the major denominations would indeed close many churches down except for the resistance of a handful of fiercely loyal parishioners. These pint-sized churches often require outside support and are a heavy drain on the denominations. Modern churches plan their seating capacity with the expectation that no more than a third of the congregation will show up at any given time, but except at Christmas and Easter, when extra services are run, the churches are still half deserted. (The long line of cars outside is deceptive. It doesn't take too many cars to create the impression of a crowd, and they may have arrived one to a customer.) At a Methodist Church I found fairly typical, Sunday attendance was as small as thirteen, and the pastor could boast only forty-five "nuclear" parishioners, out of 215 members. This church removed people from its rolls only when they had not participated in parish life in any way for *five* years.

The real issue behind membership statistics for Protestants, Catholics and Jews alike is the shallow standard of what constitutes a church member, for such standards are likely to be lower than for the average weekly ladies' bridge club. You don't really have to do much of anything to appear as a cipher in the *Yearbook*'s compilation of church members. This is what a keen observer of the American scene, Harold Laski, meant when he said that only 10 or 15 per cent of church members constitute the active core, or a Christian dissident like William Stringfellow means when he says, "The real church is very small. What we have mostly is habit, nostalgia for the past, a social form, a routinization of things." If church or synagogue attendance is any bellweather of religious conviction then the Jews certainly are in trouble as a *religious* people, for 40 per cent, according to a recent survey, never set foot inside a temple, while only 4 per cent go there weekly. It's been estimated that 25 per cent of Catholics are "nuclear," meaning that they are regular church attenders, work in the parish and accept completely the precepts of the faith. The Protestant rule of thumb is that about a third of the membership is serious about the church, a third flirts with it and the final third is made up of members in name only. A Harris poll says that out of the 91 per cent of the population who said they believed in God, only 27 per cent described themselves as deeply religious. **1452101**

If membership figures present a distorted, overblown picture of a "churchy" America, so do the polls indicating that 44 per cent of the population has attended church services within the last seven days. This "fact" is completely contrary to the experience of pastors and church authorities. The public's response to the pollsters is not subject to verification, and what the public does and what it *says* it does appear to be two different things. Evidently, people want to sound religious to be part of the popular mystique, and at work here, too, is the question of identity. Rather than climb out on an existentialist limb and say "Nothing" or "None," a person asked "What is your religion?" will answer

"Protestant," "Catholic," or "Jew," meaning his parents were supposedly of this faith, and so he, too, identifies himself. From here it's a short jump to well-meant claims of church membership and even attendance.

Aggressive, promotionally minded churches, eager to bolster their self-images and conspiring with a society which thinks that somehow it's "good" to be "religious," thus create an atmosphere of watery religiosity to which everyone is supposed to conform. During the famous "religious revival," the statistics were used almost as goads to make non-church-members feel like odd-men-out. The churches worked hard to get everyone in, no matter what their true religious concern, and the result may well have been to weaken, not strengthen, organized religion. One of the anomolous features of the current church scene is that the vast assemblage of apathetic church members will stand up and be counted on virtually one issue alone, and that is to oppose change. It seems likely that churches emphasize quantity because on the question of quality they can't be sure.

Chapter Three

Onward, Christian Elmhurst!

NOTICE OF SPECIAL MEETING

IN ACCORDANCE WITH ARTICLE 8, SECTION 2, OF THE CON-
STITUTION OF THE FIRST CONGREGATIONAL CHURCH OF ELM-
HURST (UNITED CHURCH OF CHRIST), A BUSINESS MEETING
IS HEREBY CALLED TO CONVENE IN THE MAIN SANCTUARY
OF OUR CHURCH AT 12:15 P.M., NOVEMBER 7, 1965. THE
PURPOSE OF THIS MEETING IS TO REQUEST THE RESIGNA-
TIONS OF THE REVEREND WILLIAM H. DUDLEY AND THE
REVEREND DONALD G. STONER, EFFECTIVE ON OR BEFORE
FEBRUARY 7, 1966.

ELMHURST, Illinois, lies in a greensward of Chicago suburbs with
cool arboreal names—Royal Oak, Maywood, Oak Brook. . . .
Trees push branches over wide streets, barbered lawns and hand-

37

some houses, over Elmhurst's two bars, one movie house and twenty-two churches. "A suburban town with a metropolitan atmosphere," says the Chamber of Commerce, for Elmhurst is a "bedroom town" to which many of its people return at night from the Loop, thirty minutes by Chicago and Northwestern double-decker commuter trains.

Some say that Elmhurst surreptitiously advertises the absence of Negroes and that its freedom from racial conflict is one reason real estate values are so high. Most Negroes can't afford to live in a place where the *average* income is $10,000 a year. Elmhurst, as the Chamber of Commerce announces, a little too loudly, is the "Largest City in DuPage County (Wealthiest County in Illinois and Fourth Wealthiest in the Nation)." The town, like the county, voted for Barry Goldwater in 1964. It thinks of itself as arch-Republican, stable, community-minded and religious.

Elmhurst has a Church Street, and there, or on streets immediately by, almost every Protestant denomination is represented. Steeples vie with steeples, bells with bells, pastors with pastors. Of these churches one of the least imposing happens to be the most prestigious, *the* church of Elmhurst, the old brick and stone building of the First Congregational United Church of Christ which counts among its parishioners the town's leading politicians, a good part of the country club set and some of the richest and oldest families. Late in 1965 this church, superficially peaceful, was the scene of that most undignified of Protestant spectacles, the firing of a minister.

By itself there is nothing terribly unusual in a congregation giving notice to a man of God. In some denominations, it's estimated, half the parishes are presently having trouble with their pastors, but when controversy reaches the breaking point the news is usually suppressed. In another church in Elmhurst for instance, a minister was quietly removed to a different post because he had been too active in civil rights, and the town is unaware of the reason. But at First Congregational the minister decided, as he says, "not to run," even at the risk of his career, and his fierce partisans would not let the matter rest. One of them wrote in the Christian magazine *Renewal*, ". . . there are implications . . . too significant to let die on the altar of ecclesiastical tranquility."

The Elmhurst controversy was to show just how badly divided the Christian community is on the question of what a church is supposed to be—in short, on its identity; it was to indicate that there may be in the U.S. two Protestantisms (and even two religions) in the guise of one; it was to prove how easily Christians slip into overt hostility and raise doubt as to the Christian ability to compromise and control conflict. Even if Elmhurst is a test tube, there is no reason to think that the results obtained there are not reliable. "The saddest thing of all is that the Elmhurst tragedy is not a unique or even uncommon phenomenon . . ." wrote the late theologian Dr. Fred Hoskins, reviewing the evidence in an issue of the Chicago Theological Seminary *Register* devoted to the case. "We have here word of a great sickness that is abroad. . . . I wonder if everyone who reads the Elmhurst story does not immediately identify with one or another party to the controversy. . . ."

It might be said that the question of survival brought the Elmhurst Congregationalists and Mr. Dudley face to face, and the same issue brought him down. In 1961 the parish was worried. Over the preceding three years attendance had dropped 20 per cent—from an average of 633 to 507—and the number of families pledging money dropped about the same amount. The parishioners were old and dying off—a funeral a week, it's said, was held at First Congregational—and there was no fresh body of recruits in sight. Many churches throughout the United States were having similar troubles as the "religious revival" waned, but the glowing statistics in the newspapers, inaccurate and out of date, gave the impression that religion was everywhere booming, and the Congregationalists, peering out of the narrow aperture of their own church windows, could only wonder what was wrong with them.

Eastward, in Chicago, the expanding Negro core was pushing, hurling the fleeing whites from the inner city to the suburbs, and many came to Elmhurst. The pillars of the church observed, how-

ever, that the new arrivals were not being ushered into First Congregational, and it called for an explanation. Now the real reason
appears to have been that many of the new people were not joining any church at all, but the myth of church membership, bound
up with the competitive spirit of local parishes and their largely
businessman leadership, abetted by the exaggerated claims of
other churches—subsequent Lutheran research for the town indicated the reported church membership was double the real one—
made the Congregationalists believe that the latecomers must be
going elsewhere on Church Street. There was said to be, based on
no less a statistical authority than Welcome Wagon, whose figures
showed that half the arrivals identified themselves as Catholic
("Catholics," it must be remembered, are no more likely to be
church members than "Protestants"), a Roman invasion of Elmhurst, which added to the new and unpleasant sensation at First
Congregational that the WASPs were increasingly alien, cut off,
and in the minority, their power and prestige shrinking with the
size of their church.

They needed, they thought, to be dynamic, to assert themselves
in the quest for new membership. The energizer was to be a new
minister. Such a change had been made before—in 1945 when the
parish discharged a pastor of twenty-five years standing, "amid a
fog of obscure issues and bewilderment," a parishioner recalls.
It's said that his wife ("his yoke-fellow in Christ," as ministers'
wives are sometimes called in denominational magazines) had to
be encouraged to take a trip to the hairdresser from time to time,
and her husband, a pious fellow who gave his clothes to the poor,
was similarly not quite cut out for the new affluence and sophisti-
cation of post-war Elmhurst. His successor was "permitted to
resign" in 1961. Highly competent by repute, but authoritarian,
even cold, a man with such standards of responsibility that he
brought up a mentally retarded son himself, in the parish house,
he too was thought to lack modernity and magnetism.

The new minister who came to Elmhurst at the start of 1962
had much to recommend him. He was in fact something of a

showpiece for Midwestern Congregationalists. William H. Dudley was a plain-spoken, earnest, theologically hip minister of forty-nine with a frequent smile that displayed the edge of gold on one front tooth. He was that rarity among ministers, a good preacher from the pulpit. Seventh in a successive line of ministers in his family, he had graduated from a top theological school, Yale. His twenty-seven years as pastor had been moderately successful, for each of his half-dozen churches had been a little larger and better paying than the one before. Dudley had stayed seven years at his last pulpit, a church at Cuyahoga Falls, near Akron, Ohio, and over these years the church's budget had risen from $40,000 to $100,000 annually. While some had criticized him for being too liberal, his ministry, concentrating on the importance of Christian relevance and social action, had been commended by national church officials, and other churches had offered him jobs. None, in Dudley's opinion, was sufficiently open to the sort of ministry he had in mind.

The Elmhurst pulpit committee, which came to Akron to meet Dudley and hear him preach, seemed receptive to his message, but may not have correctly gauged his seriousness. "They thought I'd be a spellbinder," he says. When the "call" came from First Congregational, with a salary of $10,000 a year plus car and house, Dudley accepted. Elmhurst, he knew, was a conservative town, but he considered it a "challenge." As he told his wife, thinking of his successful ministry in Cuyahoga Falls, "If only we could pull it off again."

It was not long, though, before Dudley and his flock began to understand that their expectations were not parallel. The minister did not want to be, as he said later, "a building manager, office worker and administrator, social director, club leader, rummage-sale promoter, pot-luck coordinator, or general master of ceremonies." His ideas about being a driving spiritual force did not include the responsibility for the church boiler, which the parishioners told him to have repaired. "That Dudley refused to look after everything was a great cause for discontent," says a psychiatrist, Dr. John W. Hanni, a member of the church under Dudley and one of his staunchest supporters. "The parishioners prided themselves on their spirit of frontier democracy but what they really wanted was a Pope to be religion for them."

It was expected, for instance, that the minister would preside over the social life of the church. First Congregational at times resembled a clubhouse where, as one parishioner put it, "people could go for a cheap evening." Take, for instance, some of its former programs for Lent and "Christian Living."

LENTEN PROGRAM

Old Testament Characters	Exploring our Christian Con-
Bowling	cerns
Ceramics	Bait and Fly Casters
Puppets	Dramatics
Desire to Join the Church	Square Dance Group
Agenda Group	Teachings of Jesus

SCHOOL FOR CHRISTIAN LIVING

Church History	Mixed Bowling
Volley Ball	Bridge Instruction
Folk Dance Instruction	"Nite of Games":
Ceramics	Ping-Pong, Shuffleboard,
Furniture Refinishing	Darts, Chess, Backgammon,
Fisherman's Hobby Group	Checkers
Courageous Living	Leather Craft
Family Church Dinners	Square Dancing
Interior Decorating	Return to Religion

First Congregational was similar to other churches in the area, the Baptists, for instance, who feature programs like "Mothers of Yesteryear," or Plymouth Congregational in nearby Maywood, which observed Maundy Thursday, conventionally devoted to "A memorial of Christ's passion," with an address by a panelist from the Darnell Institute's "Personality Plus" TV show, who spoke on "Whatever Happened to Plain Jane?" And while the Elmhurst church had largely discontinued the above programs by the time Dudley came along, the social spirit of the parish was and is enshrined by the incredible number of organizations clustered in its shadow—the Leisure-ites, the Ark (a card club), various organizations of "Christian Fellowship," the Youth Church, Couples' Club, Congregators and the Roaring Twenties.

"Elmhurst is a typical middle-class suburb with a superabundance of organizations, designated service, youth, philanthropic, and educational," said Dr. Hanni. "Many owe their origins in the past to important cultural needs, but present 'programs' are relics. One can but conclude that these organizations endure because suburban man is lonely and alienated from his neighbor. He will join damn near anything which provides even an illusion of meaningful contact. Our church was part of that culture."

Though far from being a large city, Elmhurst has over four hundred organizations, not including churches, which cater to the needs of its citizens, and the minister felt the First Congregationalists could go to them for its social life. He didn't interfere with the social circles and the bridge clubs, but neither did he stand in the doorway to nod sweetly at the needle-poised ladies or say a few appropriate words before the suppers. "They wanted me to be a front-man for religion," he says. "They wanted the sanction of the church on what they did. But I didn't want to make such functions look holy."

Bait-and-fly-casters, the Couples' Club, the Roaring Twenties and the like, you might have thought, could have gotten by without the ministerial blessing, but instead, attendance at church activities began to fall off. It was as though the members needed the minister to reassure them nothing sinful was involved in a game of bridge. The same church members who were now reluctant to attend a Nite of Games attacked Dudley bitterly for strangling them, and Christian commiseration was expressed for those who, it was said, were being deprived of their chief source of pleasure. "What do you do with people who don't *want* to join other organizations, like the ladies in their seventies? Don't we have a responsibility toward them?" And feelings ran high when Dudley reportedly characterized, on a Chicago television show,

First Congregational's social activities as, from a Christian point of view, "worthless."

"Human responsibility, engagement, is the essence," Dudley has said. These words have an existentialist flavor, but in their Christian context they come from the stream of theologians Dudley most admired—Reinhold and H. Richard Niebuhr, Paul Tillich, Dietrich Bonhoeffer and, more recently, Gibson Winter and Harvey Cox. The diverse thinking of these men can't be summed up in a few words, but generally they wanted religion to be both realistic and worldly. They were opposed to soft Christianity and false piety. The church, they said, ought to stop contemplating its own institutional navel and become relevant to the real needs of man, even if Christianity had to become "religionless," as Bonhoeffer put it. So Christianity had to become a disciplined body of believers with a purpose beyond themselves, with their eyes on the "secular city" of Harvey Cox. In this view a small number of serious Christians was infinitely preferable to a large number of social ones. They would take the theology seriously and try to make an impact on the world. In short, the locus of true religion should not be themselves.

The First Congregationalists, however, came from a different tradition, one which stressed the importance of the institution and especially the local church. In this view the denominations ought to reverse the loss in membership, provide the prophetic, socially transforming side of religion, while the local church furnishes stability and personal succor to its members. The parish has to survive, and to do this it needs new members. Dudley had been hired partly, in fact, to reverse First Congregationalist's membership losses, but shortly after assuming his post he made a shocking proposal. Instead of expanding, he said, the church should cut back even more. Out of its sixteen hundred listed members, he concluded, about one-third were seriously active, attending regularly or giving substantially or working consistently in the church's behalf, or all of these things. Another third came to church only occasionally, while the final third rarely if ever showed itself. "To be a member," Dudley says, "you really didn't have to do anything at all. You didn't even have to live in Elmhurst or nearby."

The minister's suggestion that the church cut off its dead branches met strong resistance. Some said the church institution was endangered. Before long there wouldn't be *anybody* left. To others, remembering the strongly democratic Congregational tradition, the effort seemed high-handed and dictatorial. Finally, it wasn't "Christian" to deprive a person of church membership. "We didn't like the idea of whittling down," a former trustee, a businessman, says. "We were asked to sit in judgment of others. We didn't feel we could do this as Christians. We wanted to meet the needs of humanity."

When Dudley talked about "humanity" it seemed that he usually meant the poor and the Negroes in central Chicago. When the parishioners talked about "humanity," he felt, they meant the comfortable white citizens of Elmhurst where no Negroes lived. It was a theme he plugged insistently because it involved his whole conception of Christianity and his whole reason for being a minister. The suburbanites to him were "towers of emptiness" whose only salvation was to get outside themselves and their precious routines. Exacerbated, doubtless, by the 1964 Presidential campaign—Dudley never announced his preference from the pulpit but there could have been little doubt that he was a Democrat in a Goldwater town—reactions to his sermons on social justice, the absence of Negroes in Elmhurst, and so on, were strong. "He disturbed me," says Mrs. Grace Watson, a Republican. "He didn't tell you you were great people, quite the reverse, and he gave you a jolt. I liked being unsettled—only when you are made to think is it any good going to church." To others, Dudley's hammering on the same theme was at first boring, then actively annoying. One lady called Dudley a "pulpit brat," and a professor from Elmhurst College said his sermons were "abrasive, topical, faddish." " 'Who am I? Who am I?' " a crusty old parishioner remembers. "My God, he drummed that in. We got sick of hearing it. I know damn well who *I* am. And I know that I do not come to church to be disturbed. I get enough of that in downtown Chicago during the week."

Little by little the Elmhurst parish approached civil war. Another issue was Dudley's suggestion that the church give 50 per cent of its budget for "mission"—that is, social action outside the parish. The businessmen on the Board of Trustees, seeing power slip from their hands, objected that *they* had always decided how the money would be spent. The church, they said, needed new facilities, like a parking lot, and a parish already spending 15 per cent of its budget outside its own needs could not afford to do more without risking insolvency. Once again, the minister was outvoted.

By this time the Dudleyites were thoroughly aroused. They had come to occupy many of the most important positions on the church boards. They contributed a large part of the church's budget—three of the biggest donors happened to be Dudley himself, who gave more than 10 per cent of his income, the assistant pastor, Donald G. Stoner, and the minister for Christian education, a former businessman whom Dudley had brought into the ministry at Akron and who had come with him to Elmhurst. The Dudley partisans were determined to make themselves heard. One of them, a delegate at a regional meeting of the denomination, voted in favor of a liberal resolution of civil rights which the parish had already gone on record against. Indeed, to Dudley, there was a "core" of dedicated Christians and a "periphery" of the loosely churched who swung more weight in the parish than they deserved.

Again and again the two rival notions of what a church should be met head on. As an architect named Eric Anderson told the Church Council, ". . . we have merely established a low-level, cloistered situation—an *island*. And the people on the mainland are referred to as the 'periphery.' Are we really here to sit in judgment and to agree that those on the periphery are not worth bothering about?"

Anderson, though he calls himself a conservative, recently suggested that churches in the Chicago area abandon their building programs for a year and, instead, rebuild a downtown Negro ward. But as an anti-Dudley man his eyes were on the survival of the First Congregational Church. For the parishioners were expressing their dislike of Dudley's "social gospel" by leaving the church. Membership and attendance were at record lows. Some church members withheld their contributions as a punitive measure (a step which failed to bring Dudley down because his supporters made up the deficit so that the church, for all its sorrows, had the highest budget in its history). "In fifty years," Anderson says, "Dudley might have succeeded, but in the meantime we would have had no church."

As the Christian Pandora's Box at Elmhurst opened, much was said on both sides. Dudley was criticized for refusing to make the traditional pastoral visits, for participating in civil rights demonstrations in Chicago, for making small contributions to the National Association for the Advancement of Colored People and to a white girl working for civil rights in the South. He was said to lack warmth and the ability to communicate. The Dudleyite position was made plain by Donald Stoner in a report to the church. "For it is to be recognized," he said, "that many persons are terribly threatened and almost wholly unwilling to be open to growth and change. Some express this in highly emotional and irrational ways in defense of themselves and the status quo. When this happens, tension and conflict are fuel for a destructive fire resulting in upheaval and disruption taking their toll, to the detriment of everyone concerned and certainly to the cause of Christ." In April of 1965, a special anti-Dudley committee was authorized by the Board of Deacons to conduct "a depth study among those members who wished to express their dissatisfaction. . . ." The group held meetings and contacted people by phone, and, it said, at least two hundred and seventy-five members of the congregation were unhappy: "People do not understand the sermons." "The new theology is hard to grasp. It destroys old concepts and leaves nothing in their place." The sermons put "too much emphasis on race and poverty—criticism but not comfort." "Sermons are not inspirational—too sarcastic." The Women's Fellowship, Men's Club and Leisure-ites felt that their activities were discouraged. "There is some dissatisfaction with the use of modern art in the curriculum" of the youth program. "Lack of personal warmth and friendliness on the part of Mr. Dudley and Mr. Stoner is the most frequent complaint. Members feel Mr. Dudley should *want* to make pastoral calls to become better acquainted."

There were some who felt that Dudley should have quit, following this report, on the grounds that a parish should be unified. "When a minister knows he is not welcome, if only with a substantial minority of the parishioners, he ought to have the good grace to resign," says Rev. Frederick W. Schroeder, former Dean of Eden Seminary in St. Louis, who served as interim minister after Dudley had gone. Indeed, Dudley was aware that if he stayed, fought and lost, he was unlikely to be able to continue his career as a minister, but when he suggested resignation his supporters talked him out of it. "We asked him not to leave us in the lurch," Mrs. Watkins says.

Guerrilla action and futile attempts at conciliation between the two camps continued during the summer, and then a petition was circulated and signed by seventy-four members calling for the resignation of Messrs. Dudley and Stoner. The church had been scheduled to commemorate its seventy-fifth anniversary but in view of the approaching vote it would be, said the church newsletter, "a travesty on our founders and the community of Elmhurst to celebrate anything at this time." The meeting was scheduled for November and both sides began telephone campaigns. One hundred students at Elmhurst College signed a petition supporting the ministers. Rumors were everywhere—Stoner advocated free love, Dudley had a mistress, Dudley was trying to bring a Negro family to live in Elmhurst—but the Dudley side was confident.

The meeting began after the 11 A.M. church service. Dudley, assuming there would be a debate, did not mention the matter during his sermon. Nearly five hundred people showed up. "They came out of the woodwork," Dudley says. "There were many people I had never seen before." One parishioner, pointing to Stoner, the assistant minister, asked, "Who is he?" A Congregationalist is willing to swear that he heard one man say, "I haven't been here since we fired the last minister." Memories may be colored by strong emotion, as perhaps Mrs. Watson's is when she declares, "I have never seen so many faces filled with hate." It's said, but also vociferously denied, that the congregation was in a hurry to get home to Sunday dinner and the Chicago Bear kickoff at 1 P.M. on television. (One parishioner even asserts that some showed up with portable transistors and ear plugs, but he probably saw hearing aids.)

Shortly after the meeting began a motion was made and passed to cut off debate. "Am I to be denied the right to speak?" Dudley said. "Yes!" cried a chorus of voices. The mayor, called up to give a ruling, declared that under Roberts' *Rules of Order* Dudley was indeed denied the right to speak, and the voting proceeded—245 for the resignation of Mr. Dudley, and 223 against.

From the congregation came angry outbursts and tears. Stoner, who by a narrow margin had not been asked to resign, rose to say that he was quitting anyway. Other parishioners shouted that they were leaving the church once and for all. There would be more resignations, said the moderator, and he wondered "If you realize what you have done. . . . The congregation has created its image to the community and the ministerial profession. I hope you can live with it." A student got to his feet. "Please listen to me!" he cried, but the congregation was already filing out of the aisles.

"Thirty-one years' work down the drain in an hour's time," said a Dudleyite about his pastor.

Dudley's sensibilities were bruised even further when, uncertain of his next move, he requested permission to stay on at the parsonage until he decided what to do. He could, said the trustees, at a stiff rent plus utilities. Quickly he relocated in Chicago, where he was given a job as an urban chaplain without a church by the regional office of the United Church of Christ. But his letters to the denominational headquarters went unanswered. No local congregation asked for his services, and uncertain how long the regional office would continue to employ him, he was thinking seriously of taking a job as a clerk in a department store.

"I don't think I was crucified," he told a questioner, "but I do feel there is a parallel between Christ and those who try to live the life of love and what happens to them. You have to be pretty naive and/or dedicated to stay in this profession. The First Congregational Church is typical of the United Church of Christ, which is why I will never get another pulpit. Still, I wish I could be part of people who want to grapple with life in Christian terms."

"What did we see?" wonders Dr. Percy LeFevre, Dean of the Chicago Theological Seminary. "It was a conflict born of the distance between the advanced leadership and the lay parishioner, but also the conflict was characteristic of group life when any change of a significant sort is undertaken. Dudley tried to bring an intense ministry to a congregation which was set in its ways. It didn't value the same things he did."

The happenings at First Congregational might seem like a tempest in a Protestant teapot, except that, multiplied a few hundred thousand times, it reveals a fissure with important implications, not merely theological but social and political, between those who would cling to old institutions and those who would follow a new course. Within the church such a split was inevitable, for the anti-Dudley people were prepared to resign if the voting had gone against them. As it was, about a hundred and fifty parishioners quit First Congregational, including much of the church's leadership and its heaviest contributors. Some formed the Church of the Covenant, which, though it had seven ministers in the congregation, had no salaried pastor and rented space, being utterly opposed to church buildings. With only seventy signers of its covenant, the church had a budget of $20,000, of which it gave half away, as Dudley once suggested. Meanwhile, at First Congregational, the membership stood at 1,300 and the budget at $80,000, far less than in Dudley's time. The new minister was working hard for unity. He preached love, Christian fellowship, and he did not believe a church should take a position on social issues.

An ex-First Congregationalist pointed to an article in the local paper:

MEN'S DINNER

The Men's club of First Congregational United Church of Christ, Elmhurst, will meet at 7 p.m. Wednesday, May 10, in the church. Ernest Swanson, serving as chef, will broil prime steaks for 100 men. Entertainment will be provided by a barbershop group with instrumentalists called "The Outcasts." Dinner reservations are being taken by Hugh Price and George Stauffer.

"You see," she said bitterly, "it's all back to normal."

Chapter Four

Divines in Doubt

"What is a man that thou dost visit him every morning
and test him every moment?" —JOB 7:17

THERE was a time when the minister of God felt secure about
himself, his church, and his beliefs. The occasional tremor of
doubt had passed by evensong partly because, in the end, the
clergyman could say clearly what he was. The parson was the
"person"—*the* authority in town. The rabbi was the all-purpose
expert of the Jewish community. For separation and divorce, for
business disputes, for ritual problems of menstruation and cleanli-
ness the people of the Ghetto and the Pale came to the rabbi. The
priest was certain where he stood in relation to his flock, his
superiors and God. "You are a chosen race," said St. Peter of the

clergy, "a royal priesthood, a holy nation, God's own people, that you may declare the wonderful deeds of him who hath called you out of the darkness into the marvelous light."

Today, far from feeling exalted, the clergyman is filled with self-denigration. "Ecclesiastical misfits," "macerated ministers," "gigolos for Jesus," "castrated clergymen," "occupational misfits," "prisoners of an accredited mediocrity"—in such words do ministers speak about themselves. And while the more outspoken complaints can be put down to a vociferous minority, the spiritual malaise appears to go much deeper, into the hearts of the plain-spoken preacher and the busy nun.

The clerical population of the U.S. is large—larger than most people suspect. There are 330,000 Protestant ministers (of which two-thirds function as parish clergy), 5,000 rabbis, 60,000 Catholic priests, 12,000 brothers, 175,000 sisters—about 600,000 in all, or one for every four hundred people in the country. As a group, says a psychiatrist with the Menninger Foundation, they are under greater strain than any in America, including the unemployed. Ever more frequently those who march in this small army have been asking themselves whether they are dispensable, a mere social luxury, whether the religious life is ultimately in vain. A large and growing number show the symptoms of what might be called clerical *anomie*—demoralization, rootlessness, even loss of faith.[1]

The implications of these "religious blues"—as circuit-riding Southern preachers used to call them—are enormous, for as goes the clergy so goes the church. And the clergy provided, or was supposed to provide, a sort of exemplar for America, a paradigm of the good, moral man or woman, just as the church provided, or was said to provide, moral leadership and authority. While Amer-

[1] The sociologist Talcott Parsons, discussing the problem of the anomic clergy, offers a rather more complete definition of *anomie*: "the disturbance of the state of internalized expectations of persons occasioned by the processes of change in the normative components of the institutionalized culture, and hence in the definition of what can legitimately be expected of individuals and of classes of them. The most essential point is that in the process of such change, what is expected often over such wide areas becomes seriously indeterminate."

ica still clings to the traditional image of herself reflected in her ministers' eyeglasses, the minister himself is less and less willing to be a disembodied conscience, a straight man from the American ego.

The personnel problems for modern religion begin at the beginning, that is, the seminaries. Partly, it's a question of round numbers. For the Catholics the number trouble seems greater than generally realized. Recent figures from the Midwest Religious Vocations Directors Conference showed a 30 per cent dropoff in religious candidates in the past half decade. This statistic, presented at a gloomy conference of Serra, an organization of Catholic laymen which promotes the priesthood, was followed by the observation: "There is a real crisis, and for us it is perhaps as severe—though not as dramatic—as the crisis of World War II was for the world at large."

"There is a thirty per cent decline in a lot of Catholic things," says Walter Waggoner, Executive Director of the Fund for Theological Education. Paralleling the drop in applicants are the heavy attrition rates *within* these institutions, for Catholic studies of "perseverance trends" show them heading steadily down, and there have been reported instances where 70 or even 80 per cent of a class quits the seminary before ordination. Less candidates plus more dropouts equals a projected decline of at least 40 per cent from the present level of American priests, it's thought. Robert E. McNally, S.J., of Fordham University, speaks of "the alarming rate at which the numbers of candidates for religious and sacerdotal life is decreasing. In some areas the drop is frightening. If all other factors remain constant, in the course of the next century the Catholic priesthood will almost disappear."[2]

---

[2] "Some 10,000 priests must be ordained each year, just to care for the present needs of the Church," says a report by the White Fathers, a missionary order, on the worldwide shortage of priests, "but only a little over 5,000 are being ordained in all countries. A similar situation exists for vocations in the Brotherhoods and Sisterhoods." The entire European Catholic missionary effort, the report indicates, is in extreme danger of going under because it lacks personnel.

An eminent European priest, commenting on similar difficulties there, blamed secularization and urbanization. He said that "The priesthood does not imply any longer a social promotion but rather imposes a precarious life from an economic viewpoint and does not offer the type of security which is one of the essential conditions in the eyes of modern man." Priests used to come from the peasants and the middle class, but the peasantry no longer exists and the church has had little luck with workers or service employees. As for middle class European youth, they care more for existentialism than religion. In the U.S. the situation does not appear greatly different. Among immigrant groups the priest was endowed with high social prestige but today's Catholic mother, like the Jewish, wants her son to be a scientist or doctor.

Even without a Second Vatican Council the Protestants have troubles enough with their potential clergymen. In one survey eight out of ten Protestant seminarians expressed the desire to quit. That they do not leave at the same high rate that the Catholics do is no real cause for Protestant cheer, for leaving the church after ordination is not nearly so serious for a Protestant minister as a Catholic priest, so that the decision can be deferred. More significant, perhaps, are the findings that a majority—70 per cent in one survey—of Protestant seminarians don't wish to be parish ministers, especially in small towns, a duty from which these Christian soldiers would like to be exempt. "Every theological student, every minister in fact, has worries about his vocation," says Professor James Dittes of the Yale Divinity School. "It used to be the kind of thing you confided to your roommate, but now the doubts are out in the open. It is function, though, not faith, that is in question. Everybody is searching for relevance."

This same lack of certainty is even reflected in Protestant recruitment literature: "It can be safely assumed," says a document of the NCC called *Should I Consider the Ministry?*, "that the overriding motive is the desire to lead a God-centered life and help others in church." (As we shall see, the churches themselves are far from feeling safe about these assumptions.) "Fortunate is the man who knows with absolute certainty that the occupation in which he finds himself is the only one for him. Most able people could be successful in a number of callings. The ministry is one of many options." "Options"—the language of economists and the Department of Defense—is a far cry from "the call," as St. Peter heard it, or a "Holy calling," as the Bible says.

"The seminaries," says the noted Protestant theologian, Paul Ramsey, "are populated by students who don't know if they want to go into the ministry. There has always been stress associated with aspects of the clergy, but this appears to go further; there is dissatisfaction at the very heart of it. The faith itself is in question, or at least the way faith is mediated." Much the same point was made about American seminarians by another keen observer, the British theologian Norman Pettinger: "The first thing that strikes one about the modern theological student is the degree to which he *hates* the church . . . he is very much a realist, and his realism makes him see that the organizational structures which Christian bodies must necessarily take on have become more and more an obstacle to the real work of the church. . . ."

The little world of the seminaries is really a mirror of the mature church world, of organized religion beyond. Just as the American Association of Theological Schools, in 1967, could speak of the "obsessive preoccupation of theological education with looking to the past," so the working minister often feels the churches are desperately unprepared for the present. If seminarians are frequently recruited from the bottom of the academic ladder—one church official says that 60 per cent of seminarians would have trouble getting into graduate schools in some fields— then the adult minister, as a sociologist put it, "has rapidly passed from being the intellectual doyen of society to being a member of the profession with the lowest specialist education demands. . . . The [low] level of clerical stipends is a reflection of the changing evaluation of their role—and God's role—in our society." And just as the students have profound misgivings about becoming ministers, so the ministers have misgivings about being ministers.

"Times are moving fast," writes Rev. Stephen Rose of the World Council of Churches. "Only [a few] years ago one could rationalize the increasing number of persons leaving the ministry as a revolt of mavericks. Today the disenchanted include solid biblical preachers and mature men in mid-career."

Not long ago, one of the leading Protestant journals ran a "blind ad" in the newspapers for a copy editor. A blind ad is one in which the potential employer isn't identified, so that the applicant doesn't know to whom he is writing. The editor of the Protestant magazine told me that he was surprised and extremely disconcerted to receive dozens of applications from parish ministers, some known personally to him, whom he had thought to be happy in their pulpits.

"One of the basic crises the churches face is personnel," says Rev. Ralph Peterson, former executive director of the Department of Ministers, Vocational and Pastoral Services of the NCC. The defection rate in some Protestant denominations runs about 5 per cent a year, but it must be kept in mind that a good many dissatisfied clergymen who have left the parish either work for the denominations in administrative jobs or are still carried on the rolls even though they have no functional connection with churches. Many ministers, deeply unhappy, may be afraid to say so, afraid of offending parents, parishioners, or God. I heard frequently that more ministers than their parishioners suspected stayed on only because they wanted to collect their pensions. One dimension of the church trap is that ministers, above any group one can readily think of, are unprepared for anything else, and in any case, when disillusionment sets in it may be too late. Several officials from different denominations told me they thought as many as a quarter of their ministers would leave the ministry if they had a good secular job offer with a retirement plan.

A reason so much is known about the modern minister and his troubles is that, concerned about his morale and psychological well-being, the denominations have set up clinics and study centers to help him. At such places, one hears frank talk, stripped of ecclesiastical tergiversation, about the clergyman. One such is the Institute for Pastoral Counseling, at Bloomfield Hills, Michigan. Its director, Rev. Ruell Howe, a man widely known and respected in ecclesiastical circles, has talked in depth with more than sixteen hundred clergymen from thirty-eight denominations, including Catholics. "I have been struck," Howe says, "by the contrast between the certainty of the theological student's perception of the ministry and the veteran minister's confusion about it. Some are frank to say that if they had known what it would be like, they would not have accepted ordination. There are indications that many more ministers think these thoughts but are unable to admit them."

What ails the minister? First, one expert told a top-level inter-denominational study group, is depression resulting from a crisis of faith. Citing a diagnostic program at the Menninger Foundation, he said that many ministers have no undergirding faith to support them. For many, God is dead or has no meaning, which is like a psychiatrist having no faith in the unconscious. Second, many suffer from overconstricted emotionality. Ministers were found to be unable to admit they had an aggressive side, and being unable to express the negative, the hateful, they couldn't express the positive, either. ". . . they lose their humanity; they become castrated." Third, there are the problems of the minister who said, "If the next twenty-four years are like the last twelve, to hell with it"—problems, in short, of a failure to find meaning in the ministry itself, of occupational choice. Fourth, an inability to entrust themselves to other people. The Rev. Edward S. Golden, a Presbyterian who is in charge of counseling ministers for his denomination and who made these remarks, went on to refer to the "frightening amount of apathy, inertia and vegetating" in the clerical profession.

Such insights may seem shocking for those with conventional ideas about organized religion, but they are widely borne out. Take the question of overconstricted emotionality. It seems no accident that ministers can be portrayed, almost without parody, as lackluster men in drab or old-fashioned clothes, wearing the sort of self-effacing eyeglasses that appear inevitable in the clerical profession—dark plastic on the tops of the rims and clear plastic below—so that the Bible could almost be rewritten to read, "By their dress shall ye know them." Or, more serious, the question of faith. "Many," says a confidential Episcopal report on ministers, "have doubts about their vocations as well as grave difficulties with private devotions and public worship which they feel they must keep hidden from their congregations," who are regarded by them as "enemies."

"The churches used to support a man in his doubts," says one knowledgeable churchman, "but now they are as screwed up as he is. That leaves the minister face to face, and alone, with the enemy. He has four ways to prove himself. He can be 'successful,' meaning a big budget and a lot of new members; effective, which may not be the same thing; he can have the support of powerful people; or he can deceive, or try to, about such matters as his past record when he wants to get a new pulpit."

I met a "successful" Presbyterian minister in a Southwestern city and he was a contented man. His parish is one of the largest in his denomination. He drove a Lincoln Continental with his initials on the license plate. The congregation, he said proudly, blinking behind his glasses, had just voted him a $100,000 retirement plan. His salary was over $20,000—he refused to say how much over. If membership at surrounding churches was dropping off, it was not at his, because he "beat the bushes" for new members, while other ministers were hurting themselves through being "pessimists," he said. Across town was a very different sort of Presbyterian minister. For adopting a Negro baby he had been thrown out of his Kansas pulpit. He was now the minister to a "poverty parish" of Negroes, Spanish-Americans and Indians, at the poverty-line salary of $4,500 a year. He complained bitterly of being snubbed by the rich, white churches and their ministers, especially the clergyman with the Lincoln Continental. Such contrasts, behind them serious theological contradictions, are built into American church life.

Because churches accentuate the organizational side of their existence, because the twin breasts of membership and money are constantly in front, the typical minister spends most of his time doing the very things he regards as least important. "Hence," says Samuel Blizzard, "the various offices of the ministry are normatively in one order of priority, and functionally in another order of priority. Therefore, there is much ambivalence about these offices." He concludes, "It is hard for the minister to maintain a clear vision of who he is when he is so seldom doing what he ought."[3]

For many clergymen, though, "what he ought" is far from clear. The clergyman may be touted as a "spiritual leader," given a position of honor on civic committees and a 10 per cent discount at hotels and motels, but his true function is poorly defined. With education (except for the parochial schools) handled by the state, charity by local agencies, marriages, more and more, by the justices of the peace, with midweek prayer services, evangelistic meetings and Sunday evening services on the decline, with people spending Sunday mornings driving or playing golf instead of attending church, what *is* the minister supposed to do? How can he "save souls" when the concept of "soul" barely survives?

Of course he can minister to the "spiritual needs" of his parishioners, but there's the rub. A leading frustration of ministers is that they don't like the parishioners, finding them indifferent, irresponsible and lacking integrity.[4] "They don't care about theological or social comment," I was told by a very despondent young

[3] Blizzard, in *The Christian Century*, April 25, 1956, and elsewhere identified six roles and rated them in the order ministers saw them:

Importance	Effectiveness	Enjoyment	Time
preacher	preacher	(more or	administrator (2/5)
pastor	pastor	less the	pastor (1/4)
priest	teacher	same)	preacher
teacher	priest		priest
organizer	administrator		organizer
administrator	organizer		teacher

[4] The rankings I am using are from Charles W. Steward's article, "What Frustrates a Minister?" a study of a group of middle-Western clergymen (*Christian Advocate*, Jan. 14, 1965). These same ministerial frustrations have been substantiated by many observers.

Presbyterian minister in eastern Long Island who was on the verge of quitting the church. "They want me to visit and make chit-chat, but I abhor small talk. They like a lot of illustrations, moralisms, things that are catchy. They don't make any intellectual or moral demands. They want to hear about the Golden Rule—God is love—things like that. It's a crutch for them. I try to inform them about our problems—migrant workers, open housing—but they close their eyes. I am butting my head against a stone wall." ("The church is dead and we are prolonging the funeral. Myself, I got a job, partly to get out of the parish house, and partly to establish my own identity," said his no-less-tortured wife.)

The minister's (and the church's) difficulties with function and identity might well be solved if he could lead an authentic social crusade, and so, behind the calls for relevance and action, there is an institutional imperative. This is what some Negro leaders have meant when they accuse liberal whites of needing the civil rights movement more than it needed them. Between the word and the action, however, stands the shadow of the parishioners whose conservatism in religion and politics is likely to frustrate the clergyman, if not immobilize him altogether.

The minister may be allowed, for instance, to take a strong position on civil rights if he confines himself to words, to talk about "dialogue" and the like, but he often is restrained from directed action by his parishioners. It's not usually noted by newsmen covering such events, but the religious persons demonstrating for civil rights are very often from denominational staffs and other positions where they are safe from parishioners' wrath. And when parish ministers do demonstrate, it's often away from home. One wonders if ministers ever say, "Joe, I'll do a little demonstrating in your home town if you'll take a crack at mine."

Although the clerical profession is often awarded high marks for participation in social struggles, there is strangely little evidence as to how strong the churches' influence has really been. One such study was of the racial crisis in Little Rock in 1957, and the conclusions were nothing that organized religion can brag about. "The vast majority of the city's denominational pastors were passive in 1957's crisis," the authors said,[5] and went on:

Faced with their greatest challenge, in a community in which organized liberal leadership was sorely needed to restore order while respecting the legal rights of Negro citizens, most of Little Rock's ministers assumed equivocal, cautious positions. Chaos in liberal sentiments became one of the tragedies of the fall's events. Why did the liberal ministry, reinforced by the strong stands of major religious bodies at national and regional levels, fail to become a rallying center for integrationists, as a conservative ministry had become a focal point for segregationists? The explanation lies in the nature of the ministerial role and the pressures that influence it. It seems clear that in the absence of negative reactions from their congregations many ministers would have taken effective action to secure a peaceful and numerically significant integration of the city's school facilities. Given various negative reactions, however, the minister became increasingly aware of his responsibility to preserve the church as a church, that is, to maintain church unity and with it an institutional program. Our analysis suggests that certain institutional characteristics cause the responsibility to preserve a frictionless congregation to take precedence over any desire to effectuate social reform. It further suggests that certain institutional arrangements, working propositions, communication techniques, and reactions of segregation extremists help the minister to manage his guilt while maintaining his inaction.[6]

The minister, the authors suggest, ultimately rests his case for his personal competence on how people react to his ministry, and he becomes what David Riesman called "the other-directed man." Such a personality is the polar opposite of religious teaching— imagine, for instance, an "other-directed" Christ—and it is bound to contribute mightily to still another source of the religious blues, feelings of personal inadequacy. The opinion of psychologists who have dealt with the clergy is that the minister often conceals a crisis of confidence behind these stereotyped clerical mannerisms

[5] Ernest Q. Campbell and Thomas F. Pettigrew, *Christians in Racial Crisis —A Study of Little Rock's Ministry* (Washington, D. C.: Public Affairs Press, 1959), p. 80.

[6] *Ibid.*, p. 108.

—the big, booming, reassuring laugh, the all-too-hearty hand-clasp, the excruciatingly unfunny minister's joke. ("Just talking to you, Pastor, my headache disappeared." "No, your headache didn't just disappear. Now I have it.")

"Ministers," says Dr. Howe, "are very often rigid people, definite about their faith. If anybody challenges they come to the defense of their religion. When they really don't feel secure, they start pulling their weight as ordained ministers. But secretly they are afraid of strong people and of power. Left alone in a room with a corporate director, the minister would be all nerves. If the businessman fell on the floor with a heart attack the minister would feel at home."

The low self-confidence experienced by many in the clerical profession has partly to do with their feeling of functionlessness, of doubting the efficacy of such traditional religious forms as sermons, of wondering if they are nothing more than organization men for Christ. Such ministers can end by challenging their whole being and existence. One clergyman, who now heads a group which tries to help men of the cloth in trouble, expresses the predicament:

"I ended up feeling inadequate. My whole identity got caught up in it—not just my occupation but my masculinity. You see, when I found that the identity which I had as a preacher was threatened, so was my identity as a man. I was that uncertain. So I had to back away and become not a minister, not even a Christian, but a man again. I felt I had a responsibility to myself first. All these problems of identity are exacerbated on the parish level, where I had received the most effective kind of squelch, being ignored. I went back to graduate school. I might have left the church—indeed, I still toy with the idea. There were too many things I'd come to have difficulty affirming. I couldn't pray, I didn't want to be a fraud. Lots of ministers have trouble hanging on to the traditional formulations of faith, but most go through the motions."

"Nobody today living in the parish ministry has escaped the

feeling of panic that comes with the vision of impotency," says another specialist in clergy matters, John C. Harris, Director of Clergy Training for the Episcopal dioceses of Maryland and Washington, D.C. "In the back of his mind is the knowledge that he might be an obsolescent guy. There are a number of responses. He might anaesthetize himself to the problems—the knowledge, for example, that half of his parishioners belong to the country clubs that exclude Jews. He might withdraw into himself and quietly look for other kinds of work. Or he might try to be responsible, but this is to be a sojourner in a strange land. He gets a reputation of being an odd-ball, an outcast, because he doesn't try to keep the white middle class happy."

As long as the minister was certain in his faith and secure in his position as a man of God he was able to take sacrifices in his stride. While the richer Protestant churches have begun to pay quite well—$15,000 and up, occasionally to the level of corporation presidents—the range of clerical stipends is generally low, between $4,000 and $10,000 a year, and ministers sometimes have to moonlight, especially in the poorer sections of the South. Small salaries were accepted by ministers as part of their commitment, but as commitment falters so does the willingness to accept a low standard of living. "I know as many ministers as anyone in the church, after doing clergy training for ten years," said Rev. George Peabody, brother of the former governor of Massachusetts and son of an Episcopal bishop, "and I've seen more and more leave. As the identity crisis deepens, as the job satisfaction goes down, ministers begin to feel exploited financially. Take myself, for instance. I felt the church didn't want to transform either itself or the world. I thought I had to apologize whenever I wore a clerical collar. And I began to feel trapped, finally exploited." While Peabody has not given up his Episcopal orders, he is no longer in the church's employ.

The dissatisfied and departing clergymen, without doubt, are generally those who take the idea of the relevance of religion with the utmost seriousness and are appalled by what they see as the wasteland of American churches stretching out before them. Far from being unsuccessful in their profession, they include some of the brighter ministerial lights. Some teach school; some work for the government in the poverty program; and some, unwilling or unable to sever their church connections altogether, have positions, and important ones, with their denominations or other church organizations. Most seem to cling stubbornly to a religious faith, but when it comes to conventional American church life they are potential saboteurs.

The identity crisis of clergymen is by no means confined to the Protestants. All ministers, regardless of faith, tend to function in similar ways in American churches, and just as their skills and activities are almost interchangeable, so are their problems. And so you hear a Protestant echo in the rabbi's lament: "My job is a heavy burden leading to frustration and despair. I train people in pediatric Judaism." The rabbi learns, "Ye are a kingdom of priests and a holy nation," but finds himself running a synagogue center with a nursery school, clubrooms and card tables. "The rabbi," says Nathan Glazer, "may wonder just what his function is. The Jewish law is now (except in Orthodox congregations) generally neglected, and the rabbi is no longer called upon to act as judge and interpreter. He can keep himself busy running his expanded synagogue and school and going to interfaith meetings, but does he have any role as a religious guide?"[7]

Like his Protestant peer, the rabbi often acquires his identity from the organization, and if he manipulates his role it's to become the kind of Jew the congregation wants. "I began to read avidly the registers of the seminary," says a rabbi, "I began unconsciously to memorize the names of every conservative rabbi and temple I came across . . . until I was, with all due modesty, a walking encyclopedia . . . on vital statistics in the conservative rabbinate. So that increasingly I began to accept the traits and habits of whatever I learned about the personalities of individuals

[7] Nathan Glazer, *American Judaism* (Chicago: Univ. of Chicago Press, 1957), p. 125.

as a standard to imitate. And, actually, I molded myself into one of them before I knew it."[8]

One might suppose that because, unlike his Protestant brethren, the rabbi has a double role, not only as a spiritual leader but as an ethnic functionary, he would be sustained in his work despite the dissatisfactions. And while there does not seem to be the same order of ferment as in Protestantism or Catholicism, Jewish leaders do talk of the shortage of rabbis, teachers and cantors, the disinclination of rabbinical students to become rabbis, and the desire of rabbis to leave the parish. One well-known rabbi who made this step is Arthur Gilbert, now of the Anti-Defamation League. "Many rabbis would prefer other kinds of work if it were available," he says. "I found myself as a rabbi being a rentable commodity. I was rented for marriages, counseling, funerals and so on. It was the major part of my ministry, even though many of those I served were not of my own congregation. Every evening included a visit to a bereaved family, and it was a rare Sunday I didn't have to switch emotions as I went from a wedding, to a baptism, to a funeral, and then to a young adult dance. It wasn't the way I wanted to use myself and my learning. As I look back on it, I can see that death took precedence over everything. I found myself incapable of responding. I began to resent."

But the straying of ministers out of the local parishes and out of the churches altogether goes on quietly, unpublicized. It is the Catholic priest and nun who make the headlines, partly because the commitment they make is seemingly so total, and partly because it is wondered if the unshakable monolith of the Catholic Church is tottering. Just how many Catholic religious are actually defecting is a mystery. Authoritative Catholics say that a proposed investigation into the question, several years ago, was blocked at the highest American levels, but the real problem in obtaining figures is the Catholic organization itself—148 dioceses and archdioceses, many hundreds of male and female orders

[8] Lee Brande, "The Rabbi: Some Notes on Identity Clash," *Jewish Social Studies*, XXII (January, 1960), 4352.

(there are, counting small ones, 443 orders of Catholic women in the U.S.), all semi-autonomous and apparently not too eager to confide even in one another. According to Father David P. O'Neill, ". . . the number of priests who fail, leave the service of the Church to undertake other work, and, often enough, contract civil marriages, is far more than is popularly imagined. Priests are normally loyal to one another as well as to the Church, and they help in every way to cover up the public disgrace and unfavorable publicity that may arise when one of their number gives up the practice of the priestly vocation. For this reason no reliable statistical studies seem to be available on this problem."[9]

The clandestine departure of priests into matrimony, remarks a Protestant magazine rather tartly, has become so commonplace that the proper place to mention it is in the weddings section, not the news. One story has it, about a monastery suffering heavy defections, that as each brother left his name was scratched from the list. One day a note on the roster said, "Will the last one out please blow out the sanctuary lamp and make sure the windows are locked?"

It is clear that sisters are leaving the religious communities—sometimes to set up groups of their own which still observe the laws of poverty and chastity—in record numbers, for there were, by official tally, four thousand fewer sisters in 1967 than in 1966. The situation for priests is murkier, partly because the names of priests are often carried, sometimes for years, on Catholic rosters after they have left the church, on the grounds that they are still making up their minds. The usual estimate of ex-priests in America is five thousand as compared to a priestly population of sixty thousand. Some Catholic spokesmen think that both the figure and the talk about a mass exodus of priests is the invention of sensational journalists, but others believe the true number of priestly renegades may well be higher. One such is the priest-sociologist, Joseph Scheuer, co-author of *The De-Romanization of the Ameri-*

[9] David P. O'Neill, *Priestly Celibacy and Maturity* (New York: Sheed and Ward, 1965), p. 43.

can Catholic Church, who says that the defection rate is "fantastic, and in addition you must count as potential leavers a hell of a lot of misplaced priests." William Restivo, an ex-priest who set up an organization called Bearings for Re-Establishment (which tries to find jobs for "fallen" priests and sometimes has a difficult time when potential employers are Catholics), thinks there will be closer to fifteen thousand of them. And it should be noted that the departed are coming from the upper reaches of the church structure, not simply parish priests but theologians, monsignors and leading Catholic educators alike.

"The institutional church is in trouble," says Monsignor Ivan Illich, director of the Center of Intercultural Documentation in Cuernavaca, Mexico. "The very persons on whose loyalty and obedience the efficiency structure depends, increasingly abandon it. Until the early 1960's, the 'defections' were relatively rare. Now they are common. Tomorrow they may be the pattern. After a personal drama played out in the intimacy of conscience, more and more ecclesiastical employees will decide to sacrifice the emotional, spiritual and financial security which the system benevolently provided for them. I suspect that within this generation these persons will have become a majority of the Church's personnel."

It is not astonishing that the Catholic Church, which has institutional as well as religious reasons for doing things, describes the current defection in terms flattering to itself. After all, there are fresh priests to be recruited to replace those who have left. So the ex-priest is referred to as "derelict" or "fallen," obviously from a higher place to a lower one (Satan's fall?), and the descent is thought to represent the elimination of undesirable elements. Some of those who have done the dropping have few kind words for the church. Charles Davis, the English theologian who departed the priesthood to marry, called the Catholic Church "at best irrelevant and at worst an obstacle to genuine human experience." For one priest in trouble with the authorities, "The church is quite plainly corrupt."

A thirty-five-year-old defected priest I talked with spoke of the "prisonlike atmosphere" of the church and its "institutional inflexibility." Celibacy, he said, was not a strain "when you are involved with people all the time," though it was a lonely life. Having decided to leave, he said, "for the first time in years I began remembering my dreams, a sign I was no longer repressing anything." He had strong objections to stipend and stole fees—that is, fees charged by priests for special prayers and the like—but most important "the Catholic faith is the system and I lost faith in the system." Uncertain what to do, he took a leave of absence and, in civilian clothes, on borrowed money, hitchhiked around the U.S., "searching my way. Wherever I went I'd talk to people and before long priests and nuns were contacting me. Many said they would like to get out of the church. I feel many—no, I would say most—priests are radically discontent."

Indeed, once it became permissible to criticize the Roman Church, after Vatican II, a battery of clerical objections was aimed at it. Father Joseph Fichter, a noted Catholic sociologist, discovered that 62 per cent of priests responding to his poll favored the diocesan priest's freedom to marry, which meant, he said, that they want to remove celibacy—which the Vatican calls "the heavy and sweet burden," the "total" gift to God—as a condition for ordination. Priests felt trapped in inefficient organizations which subjected them to petty regulations, did not utilize their talents and blunted their zeal. Startlingly, said Father Fichter, a large proportion of men favored "some form of honorable exit from the priesthood, a negative attitude that is necessarily bound up with the unsatisfactory career pattern for the priesthood."

And, says an outspoken priest in the Steubenville *Register*, a diocesan newspaper, "Despite what magazine articles say and popular fancy might think, the chief vices of the clergy have been ambition and the selfishness on which it feeds. . . . Only in the most intimate clerical circles is there any awareness of a decline in quality. . . . The church will survive, of course, but only because

God has promised it will; and survival will be in small groups of the elect, not in the magnificence that is her proper heritage as the Mother and Teacher of the whole world."

To an outside observer, one of the most interesting features of the Catholic Church scene is the loyalty which it has been able to command from its religious personnel. It must almost seem, at times, to those within the church organizations, that customs are specifically designed as a perpetual test of faith, for clearly the restrictions must seem onerous, at least to independent spirits. Sisters' mail is sometimes censored and, in some orders, a sister can go home for the death of a parent but not a grandparent! One order of sisters was directed by a bishop to retire by 10 P.M., "so as to have adequate sleep." "The requirements [for reading] are to be carefully observed. A reading list is to be prepared, with the advice of our representative, for use in table reading in all houses of the congregation." The sisters were not to be out of the convent after 8 P.M. They were forbidden to eat at people's homes, and were told to avoid unnecessary conversations with the laity. If conversations sometimes couldn't be avoided, there definitely "are to be no particular friendships with the laity. The sisters are not to engage with members of the laity in forms of recreation inconsistent with the reserve which belongs to their religious form of life."

One sister, the president, no less, of a Catholic college, has to put in a requisition if she wants to have her shoes repaired! Travel is an enormous difficulty—the sisters not only have to ask for the money but obtain permission, on forms submitted in quadruplicate, for every stay along the route. Sister Charles Borromeo, a respected Catholic intellectual who was attached to the Vatican Council as an observer, explains some of the practical problems of a sister's life. "Sisters disagree as to whether the habits are uncomfortable. I have known sisters who have had abscessed earlobes for twenty-five years because of the cowl. It's hard to hear through four layers of cloth. Your vision is restricted. The heavy cloth is hot and quite hard to keep clean. Underneath their habits sisters wear T-shirts. They use men's handkerchiefs and wear heavy masculine shoes. The idea, of course, is to change a woman's drive to have unique garb into a stylized form. It's a kind of people-control, to alter your name, cut off your hair, change your clothes and give you a laundry number. The men are put in skirts and cassocks, so that both are desexualized. The accent is always on the externals—how you walk or avert your eyes. The formation, far from forming us, was what we fought. Anybody who bought the formation—six years of training, isolation, withdrawal, exposure only to people of your own age and sex—was deficient. Anybody who is objective today hasn't bought the system. She accepted it for larger ends. Today the sisters under thirty-five are asking questions. Anybody who isn't asking questions is neurotic. The religious life today is a horror. The set-up is unhealthy."

A confidential study to the Vatican from a bishop, about which more will be said in the next chapter, lists five major problem areas of the Catholic clergy. First, authority, partly due to structure and partly to how priests and sisters internalized it; second, sex, including, for priests, the acting out of unresolved relationships with women and the lack of capacity to respond to affection; third, addiction, such as alcoholism; fourth, loss of faith; and finally, status, accentuated by changes going on in the world.

Secret reports, polls, defiance of bishops by priests, clerical unions, seminarians on strike, dark questions about papal infallibility, dropouts—it can't be said that the Catholic authorities are unaware of the ferment. What aggravates the issue even further is that a failure to execute far-flung change risks a much higher defection rate than the church is already experiencing. And yet the indications are that the Catholic Church, like the Protestant, will find change excruciatingly slow, often all but impossible. For the risk of change will appear, to the church organizations, as greater than that of remaining more or less the same. So the Pope reaffirms the celibacy laws in no uncertain terms, and in Chicago an order of nuns, experimenting with individual garb, without headgear, plaintively asks the papers not to report on it for fear of bringing down the diocesan wrath.

Institutional and psychological reasons argue for the status quo.

Celibacy, for instance, can't be divorced from its setting—the Catholic residence, geared to single men, and the wage scale which would have to be drastically raised to provide for family incomes. Catholic schools and hospitals depend on the free labor of nuns— it is said to cost the church only $1,500 a year to keep a nun— and if they were to be secularized, even married, expecting normal salaries, many Catholic institutions would have to close their doors. But even if such difficulties could be hurdled, the church would still be confronted with that large group, in the clergy and out of it, whose religious expectations are entirely traditional and whose unquestioning support might well be lost—like the sisters whose identity is attached to their habits. ("Who would they be without them?" a sister asked contemptuously.) The church's own identity, moreover, as its function becomes less and less clear, is increasingly established by the customs and beliefs which mark it off as something separate. The Catholic Church, then, appears to be trapped between those who cry for relevance, for a sweeping revision in traditions to make them contemporary, and those for whom custom *is* the church. Every major step toward change is bound to be fought and probably defeated by a powerful rear guard.

This traditionalistic side of the Catholic Church was made palpable for me by a visit to a convent of cloistered nuns. The Mother Superior was a small, birdlike woman of indeterminate age. Her gestures were childlike, her voice tiny, high and serene. Her steel-rimmed eyeglasses peered through a metal grating separating us. One knew, of course, of such a life, but still it was a shock to encounter it. No one passed in or out of the sanctuary. The doors opened only from the inside. Food was passed through turnstiles. The nuns rose at 5 A.M. for prayer, and prayed a dozen times a day—"The entire day is a prayer," said the handbook—at the summoning of bells, to Lauds, Matins, the Holy Sacrifice of the Mass, the Hours of Terce, Sext and None, the Vespers, the community Rosary, mental prayer and Compline, and in addition there were private "privileged" intervals in chapel. Ceaseless activity consumed the remaining hours, and though the sisters were permitted to break silence in their social period I wondered what they had to talk about, since they had no access to news or contemporary literature. They fasted and slept on boards. Periodically, the Mother Superior explained, with a sideways glance, they used the "discipline," scourging themselves on their "lower parts." (They were spared, however, the sharp chains which constantly prickle and sometimes draw blood, still worn about the arms by nuns in some convents.) These sisters were allowed one night a week of unbroken rest, but, said the Mother Superior, they often chose to rise on those nights, too. On other nights the sisters roused themselves for the horarium, at midnight, for a silent, hour-long vigil, because this was the "evil hour," the Mother Superior told me, for the world.

A third of the women were over sixty-five and had been there most of their lives. All would stay until they died, their existence fixed and unchanging, in a relentlessly similar pattern, repeated day after day. I asked, perhaps rudely, if the sisters were ever bored, and the Mother Superior answered, using a phrase I had thought extinct, "How could there be boredom for a bride of Christ?"

It was wrong, she said, to suppose that the life was suffering. Rather it was joy—joy in giving of oneself.

"And does your life have a meaning for our contemporary world, Sister?"

"Of course! We preserve an ideal."

The priest who had brought me there shook his head sadly as we walked away. "Well," he said slowly, "suppose they do preserve an ideal. But what does it mean? And how can they communicate it when nobody knows they are here? Preserve it for whom?"

Chapter Five

The "Sick" Clergy

For a priest is a miracle of God's love to us; a man
who, through His Sacrament of Ordination becomes
another Christ with powers that beggar human imagi-
nation. . . . Nothing can be greater in this world of
ours than a priest. Nothing but God Himself.
A priest is a holy man because he walks before the
Face of the All Holy.
A priest understands all things.
A priest forgives all things.
A priest is a man who lives to serve.
A priest is a man who has crucified himself, so that
he too may be lifted up and draw all things to Christ.
A priest is a symbol of the Word made flesh.
A priest is the naked sword of God's justice.
A priest is the hand of God's mercy.
A priest is the reflection of God's love.
He teaches God to us. . . . He brings God to us. . . .
He represents God to us.[1]

IT is a measure of how rapidly the world of American religion is
changing that the above "job description" of a priest, written only
twenty years ago, already sounds as though it belongs to another
age. The churches no longer want to seem perfectionistic, even

[1] Catherine de Hueck, *Dear Seminarian* (Milwaukee: Bruce Publishing Co.,
1950), pp. 85-87. Quoted in Margaretta K. Bowers, *Conflicts of the Clergy*,
(New York: Thomas Nelson and Sons, 1963), p. 10.

74

pietistic; they would rather appear natural, attractive, down-to-earth: "Try saying 'Nazareth College.' There! You must admit it has a rather nice ring to it." "How is Jesuit education like a Volkswagen? Dependable—keeps good things and basic designs for basic needs—first things first—recognizable everywhere." Or priestly recruitment literature: "It's a great life!"

Religion still believes in the call from on high, but more and more, psychological examinations are required to see if the person heard it right. There has been a subtle shift away from what Protestant research describes as a "special leading" where "God enters directly into human affairs and causes His works and His will to be unmistakably evident above the background 'noise' of normal life and in addition to His own general providence," toward a leading identified as "natural," meaning that God is remote and, in the absence of breathtakingly clear signals, an individual must find his own way.[2] The zealot with an intense religious leading is regarded with suspicion by modern seminaries and probably rejected.

Clergymen are being increasingly examined today by the churches for signs of poor mental health, and for three important reasons. The first is the fear, usually unspoken but prevalent, that the men and women attracted into the clergy often come from the neurotic side of the population. The second is the worry that if the whole population—not just clergymen—shows a strong neurotic streak, the strains and stresses of clerical life are enough to bring a quiet neurosis to the boiling point. And the third is the conviction that, when organized religion is in a testing time, when it is under fire from without as well as within, the churches will need the most mature, best-adjusted and self-reliant people they can get.

Just as the notion of curing the soul is vanishing from religion, so the minister is no longer exempt, by virtue of his divine connection and special grace, from being gauged according to ordinary

[2] Frederick R. Kling, *The Motivation of Ministerial Candidates* (Princeton, N. J.: Educational Testing Service, 1959), pp. 12 ff.

standards of adjustment. But if the churches have been amazingly frank and open in their private appraisals, they have been less than eager to publicize the results, apparently through fear of tarnishing the religious image and the faith people have in it. Not many Episcopalians know, for example, that there has been in existence since the early 1960's a Bishops' Commission on Pastoral Counseling whose name was rather deliberately selected to conceal the true interest of the bishops and the psychoanalysts working with them—the incidence, thought to be high, of homosexuality, alcoholism, and chronic marital troubles among the Episcopal clergy, along with widespread "vocational disenchantment."

Most clergymen of the various faiths, needless to say, are not alcoholic or homosexual. On the other hand chronic marital discord in some denominations is said to be considerable, although, as one church official told me, "Ministers will cover it up, and settle for a low level of happiness, just like junior executives will, for the sake of their careers." But enough clergymen have these problems to cause concern, and beyond the slippery labels of neuroses there are enough inwardly tortured people in the clergy to make church authorities wonder what in heaven is wrong.

The scientific examination of ecclesiastical mental health can be traced to the work of Thomas Vernon Moore, a student of medicine and psychiatry and a priest who served in no less than three religious orders. He joined the last, the Carthusian, at the age of sixty-five, and became a founder of the order in this country. Moore published a paper in 1936 in which he said that the "excess" of *dementia praecox* might be accounted for by the tendency of pre-psychotic personalities to seek out the religious life. As he put it, ". . . evidently an undue proportion of individuals who, to say the least, are paranoid personalities, seek admission to the priesthood."[3]

Within the inner sanctums of the Catholic Church, Moore's

---

[3] Thomas V. Moore, "Insanity in Priests and Religious," *Ecclesiastical Review*, 2 (1936), 484-498 and 605.

results caused dismay and controversy. Some feared a blemish on the priesthood, while others felt that using scientific techniques to examine those with a supernatural calling was profane and blasphemous. More recently the objections have come from the other side, from social scientists who believe that Moore's methods were faulty and produced too pessimistic a picture of the priesthood. But Moore's findings were generally correct, says Father William C. Bier, head of the department of psychology at Fordham University, a man who has done much to win the battle for Freud in the American Catholic Church (although the battle for Catholic psychiatry remains undecided). "Father Moore suggested that very likely it was a matter of pre-selection," Bier says, "that the religious and especially the contemplative life exercise a fascination for those predisposed to mental illness. But the religious life contributes too by making strong demands. Moore inferred that the religious life affected the psyche and produced mental illness. The vows are noble but in keeping them some people pay a price."

Although Moore specifically excluded celibacy as a cause of mental illness, many later writers think it takes a toll. ". . . priests in some proportion, much larger than commonly thought, do suffer in their inner personal life, and in the quality of their work and service for the Church, from a lack of understanding and adjustment to their celibacy," says Father David P. O'Neill. "Added to these are those many priests . . . who fail altogether to live out their lives in celibacy, and retire from the work and life of the Church. . . . The number of priests involved in these two groups is clearly more than sufficient to justify honest, open and expert examination of the celibacy law. . . ."[4]

[4] O'Neill, *op. cit.*, p. 56. Fr. O'Neill, as it happens, is a cautious defender of priestly celibacy. But he wishes it to be understood in modern terms, and uses Freud for his authority. Freud (who regarded religion as obsession-compulsion neurosis) is said by Father O'Neill to have had sexual development in mind, in the fullest sense, not just the sexual act. Sexual development to Father O'Neill is the capacity for full affective expression. Celibacy is not abnormal then but can be mature sexual expression if properly understood not as deprivation but enrichment. A nun goes even further: "The orgasm is not

About half of today's priests attended minor as well as major seminaries, which means that they were cloistered from their fourteenth to their twenty-fifth years. (In Europe, the cloistering sometimes started at age ten.) Dr. Bernard E. Hall, a psychiatrist with the Menninger Clinic, has said that clerical dropouts will increase because candidates choose the clerical life for the wrong reasons, as a defensive maneuver against "unmanageable upsurge of sexual and aggressive impulses." The delusion that sexual impulses would disappear, he said, could be carried on for years, but "to accept as a fact a fourteen-year-old boy's statement that he wants to be a priest and take the vows of chastity, poverty and obedience is ridiculous."

The probings of the Catholic Church into its personnel did not simply happen spontaneously but were brought about at least partly as an organizational necessity, just as those who call for married priests justify their argument by saying that in no other way will the church have priests. The necessity, of course is the high rate of discontent and leaving. The Pope has admonished seminary directors to weed out potential malcontents, and Catholic seminaries now use psychological tests and interviews to try to decide who will make a weak or ex-priest later on. For the church the results are not encouraging.

---

the greatest love between man and woman. There are possibilities for sexual communion and completion which the orgasm cannot reach. This seems to be the profound implication that lies at the foundation of Christianity. The virginal depth of human sexuality is yet to be discovered in all the impact of its splendor." This is frank talk for Catholics, who still almost always refer to sex as "marriage." Neither of these attempts to make celibacy seem normal and natural is convincing. Better is the argument that it is simply an act of faith.

Still another example of the Catholic approach to sex is found in the writings of Marc Oraison, the French priest-physician whose modernistic ideas have not found favor at the Vatican. Modern he may be, but he still refers to adolescent masturbation as "autoerotic regression," an idea not shared by any modern secular authority. Father Oraison talks about the "mystery" of sexuality," relating it to the religious mystery, as though sex still needed some justification in terms of ultimate meaning. This search for ultimate meaning in general has been given up by many secularists as an unrewarding enterprise, and marks a clear line between religious and non-religious thinkers.

One such study was made by Dr. Walter Coville, a psychiatrist who screens religious candidates in the dioceses of New York City and Rockville Center, Long Island. In an analysis of 107 male major seminarians, Coville discovered that 8 per cent were sexually deviant and another 70 per cent were described as "psychosexually immature, exhibiting heterosexual retardation, confusion concerning sexual role, fear of sexuality, effeminacy, arty interests and potentially homosexual disposition. The effects of this problem on personal adjustment and peer relationships in the religious life and its long-range effect on the image of the priest or religious are a source of grave concern to administrators. . . ."[5]

"Arty interests" would seem to reflect the church's desire to be four-square, red-white-and-blue, he-man American, but Coville's results, if representative of seminarians at large, do not suggest that the church is attracting such people, if indeed they exist. Coville also identified 50 per cent of the seminarians he studied as "passive-dependent," defined as "helpless and indecisive, tend to cling to others, and engage in one-sided relationships." This type "is attracted to the structure of the religious life, initially adjusts well in it, but later becomes quite troublesome and may develop serious adjustment problems." He goes on, "I am impressed in my own work with candidates for the religious life with the high incidence of emotional immaturity and insecurity; with the great number of young men and women who frankly admit that they fear to make decisions, want to avoid responsibility and prefer to be 'followers.' "

"In the best of situations," Coville told me, "the priesthood is a profession that calls for stable people."

Still other studies of applicants to the Catholic clergy point to the patterns identified by Dr. Coville. One, of women in training for the sisterhood, considering them by "suitability," was able to rate only 32 per cent as excellent or good, with the others de-

[5] Walter J. Coville, "Basic Issues in the Development and Administration of a Psychological Assessment Program for the Religious Life." Unpublished paper.

scribed as fair, weak or needing more than normal guidance.[6] Another, comparing college women and women religious applicants, found the latter to show higher introversive and perfectionistic tendencies.[7] Yet another study concluded, "Thus a summary of more than fifteen years of research seems to confirm the findings of the pioneer studies of the early forties that religious and religious applicants show signs of defensive behavior typical of persons with neurotic tendencies."[8]

A British expert in religion describes the church as an "inverted pyramid, with the aged majority at the top and a young minority at the bottom." Pointing to the numerical decline in the priesthood, he said that "it is the insecure young men who are prepared to accept authority, rather than the radical. . . . Your men who are looking for security, who are basically afraid of ideas, who lack initiative—these are the ones that remain."[9]

Indeed, the Catholic opposition to psychoanalysis may have more than theological grounds, for in a Benedictine monastery in Mexico where analysis was required for monks, a large percentage, after talks with the analyst, decided to leave the order. The prior, Father Gregoire Lemercier, was ordered at last by the Vatican to stop using psychoanalysis in the monastery, with the result that the entire twenty-one-man order that was left quit the monastic life to set up a psychoanalytic-based community of their own, with no ties to the Catholic Church.

The Catholic hierarchy ought not to be unmindful of the problem of neurosis among its clerics, for it was clearly stated in a document prepared for the Bishop of Cuernavaca, Mexico, which has received wide circulation in high American church circles. "Psychological studies," the report says, "show a strong sampling

[6] John J. Rooney, "Psychological Assessment on a Community of Teaching Sisters," *The Catholic Psychological Review*, 4, No. 1 (Spring, 1966).
[7] Mother Elaine Sandra, "Degree of adherence to the Catholic religion as related to selected personality indices." Unpublished doctoral dissertation, Fordham University, 1957.
[8] R. Dunn, "Personality Patterns among Religious Personnel: A Review," *The Catholic Psychological Review*, 3, No. 2 (1965), 125-137.
[9] *National Catholic Reporter*, June 7, 1967.

in religious and clerical life of the withdrawn, docile, overly sub-
missive personality together with a growth in the troublesome,
aggressive personality, suggesting that the choice of religious and
clerical life might be for many a misguided way to resolve a
psychological problem in the area of obedience and authority."[10]

The report also has a good deal to say about sexual problems,
referring to "occasional or quasi-habitual (chronic) deviation,
whether it be heterosexual, homosexual or masturbatory" and
"laxity with regard to erotic thoughts, desires, reading, shows,
etc." The problem of unresolved relationships with women is
thought to be the most frequent among the clergy and "spells out a
simple lack of maturity with regard to this vital human relationship." The report talks about "latent homosexuality and unresolved Ocdipal impulses" and it says, "Many young men burdened
in this way find their way into religious and clerical life, not only
because they are typical products of our culture and of the present
conditions of family life, but also because religious or clerical life
offers to many of them an apparent solution to their problems."

It would seem, then, that certain kinds of Catholics are attracted into the religious life structure because of the way that
structure is built, and the church not only satisfies their needs but
reinforces them. As a churchly cliché has it, the church makes
boys out of men. Consider the seminary system. The early church
in America had no seminaries, but, as a largely immigrant church,
it did have a ghetto mentality and when seminaries were built they
were put in isolated rural areas, partly because of the frontier but
mostly because it was thought that freedom from distractions and
temptations was good for piety. With physical came mental isolation, and there are still a few seminaries in which the reading of
anything not published by the Catholic press is forbidden. Seminarians ate, prayed, slept at the same time, always under supervision. Protected, sheltered, immunized from the world, the semi-

---

[10] "Report on Materials Submitted to the Bishop of Cuernavaca, Mexico,
with Respect to Conflict-Situations for Priests in the Modern World." Unpublished paper.

narian's "social and personality development is definitely slowed."[11]

"A great mass of psychological 'testing,'" write two priest-psychologists, Eugene C. Kennedy and Paul F. D'Arcy, "has revealed a curious truth about the typical American seminarian. While he has a great desire to help other people, he has a built-in difficulty making easy relationships with them. . . . He is shyer and more self-conscious than his peers. Sometimes . . . seminaries merely reinforce what he is good at [self-control] by insisting on practices which further inhibit the very development he needs." They are frank to say that separation, detachment, aloofness and silence can create an abnormal attitude in which "the normal person in religion is made to feel guilty because he cannot lead an abnormal life perfectly. On the other hand, abnormal people are not only tolerated but rewarded because they can lead an abnormal life almost perfectly."[12]

William Restivo, the former Catholic priest who set up Bearings for Re-Establishment in New York to help ex-priests find work, says they have trouble getting jobs, partly because Catholics discriminate against them, partly because it's suspected they must be unreliable, or worse, alcoholic or homosexual, and partly because they are not just inexperienced but defensive and very naïve because of their seminary training. "We are not taught to relate to people but to God," Restivo says, "and a person who comes out of seminary has a hard time with people. His emphasis has been so much on the inner, spiritual life, which is considered of a much higher order."

It is true that the seminaries are slowly changing. Minor seminaries are being de-emphasized, and modern-minded major seminaries have begun to relax the rules and supervision to encourage greater self-reliance. The Jesuits not long ago abandoned an al-

---

[11] Safford Poole, *Seminaries in Crisis* (New York: Herder and Herder, 1965), p. 73.

[12] Eugene C. Kennedy and Paul F. D'Arcy, *The Genius of the Apostolate* (New York: Sheed and Ward, New York, 1965), p. 61.

most new, multi-million-dollar seminary in the rural East to rebuild it in an urban area. But many informed Catholics agree with Father Safford Poole that "the seminary system is the Achilles' Heel of American Catholicism" because the change *is* so slow. Evidently, too, there are limits to how far a seminary can change and remain a Catholic seminary, a preparation for the Catholic religious life.

The Catholic religious environment is thus said to be congenial to passive and sexually confused people, and those who as priests develop alcoholism and severe personality problems could be matched, Father Poole says, "with one whose sexual confusions have been borne without outside professional help, by one whose ignorance has wreaked havoc in the confessional or counseling parlor, and by one who is lazy, indifferent, frustrated or just plain defeated by it all."[13]

"Strictly speaking," writes a Catholic authority on the subject, "the Church has the right to inflict corporeal punishment, such as fasting and imprisonment, though she does not use such penalties today." I visited a modern refuge for alcoholic priests called Guest House Sanitarium, near Lake Orion, Michigan, a suburb of Detroit. There are several such facilities in the U.S.—one in New Mexico, one in Wisconsin. Known as *refugia peccatora*, their existence for years was a closely guarded secret of the church, as though acknowledging such problems would defile the Catholic name. The other *refugia*, which treat sex and disciplinary problems as well as alcoholism, are little better than prisons, I was told at Guest House. But here, on a large and lovely estate, the priests, twenty or thirty at a time, alcoholics all, have the most modern treatment and facilities. Alcoholism is not regarded as a manifestation of Original Sin but as a bio-chemical imbalance fed by anxiety and emotional insecurity, to be greeted not by punishments and threats of Hell but by understanding and psychiatric care.

Guest House was started in 1951 by Austin Ripley, a former

[13] Poole, *op. cit.*, p. 29.

newspaper man who recognized the problem, thought something should be done about it, and raised the money for the sanitarium himself. Ripley has had long experience with the alcoholics of the apostolate, and he guesses that somewhere between 5 and 10 per cent of priests can be classified as alcoholic, a rate somewhat higher than that of the general population. He feels that the alcohol problem is increasing among priests under the impact of change in the church and expects the number of alcoholic clerics to double as the pressures rise. Celibacy is an issue for some, but only for some, Ripley emphasizes, while for others authority is the bane. "For a great many priests," Ripley said, "the problem is not lack of freedom within the Church, but the fear of exercising the freedom and rights they have. I predict the Church will see more alcoholic priests in the next five years than it has in the last seventy-five."

One priest at Guest House told me that he had been "stuck" in a small Ohio town for eighteen years. Living, he said, in conditions approaching squalor, lonely, for he was the only priest in town, roused by his parishioners at any hour of night, he detested his parish and felt completely forgotten by the church. But instead of asking for a transfer to a larger parish, as he wanted, he sulked, drank and ended in a sanitarium.

The indelible impression is that a great many Catholic clergymen entered the priesthood for psychological as well as spiritual reasons—such as not having to exercise freedom or prove themselves in sex. Here, Protestant researchers strongly echo the Catholics. A New York psychiatrist named Gotthard Booth, for instance, studied postulants of the Episcopal Diocese of Newark and the General Theological Seminary of New York. In the ideal case, he said, the religious candidate would be attracted by the ideal aims of the church, but in reality all candidates are influenced by "nonspiritual needs" and some attracted excessively by worldly ego gratifications offered by the Episcopal priesthood. Among those he mentioned are conspicious social dignity for men from poor families or who suffer from strong feelings of inferiority, security for those who had little parental affection at home and who can find it in the family atmosphere of the church, and a cover for homosexuality which may not be overt or even conscious but for which the church offers a place where celibacy isn't suspect, where men can wear quite feminine clothes, or where aggressive people of this type can feel secure wielding power for the good of the church. Finally, Booth listed the emotional and aesthetic side of the services. The priesthood, he said, offers one of the few places in American life where participation in aesthetic-emotional events is socially acceptable—that is, not considered "queer."

The psychiatrist stirred a controversy when he said that for such people the church provides a place to function effectively, when they might have broken down in other situations. And he was convinced that the church would be deprived of some of its best men if they were thrown out.[14] (Congregations have sometimes proved more tolerant than one might suppose. A Protestant minister in Arizona ran off with a male concert pianist but when he returned his parish took him back.)

The concern today is that while passive-dependent and other "neurotic" clergymen might have thrived in the secure church structures of the past, they will have a harder time doing so in the future, in shakier churches with weaker identities, where the very ambiguities of the ministerial profession call for a high ability to "take it." Many clergymen seem to stand on that slippery, shifting terrain which Allen Wheelis calls "the loss or impairment of identity. Identity can survive major conflict provided the supporting framework of life is stable, but not when that framework is lost. One cannot exert leverage except from a fixed point. Putting one's shoulder to the wheel presupposes a patch of solid ground to stand on. Many persons these days find no firm footing; and if everything is open to question, no question can be answered."[15] The churches, it would seem, fail to offer firm ground, and those al-

[14] Gotthard Booth, "The Psychological Examination of Candidates for the Ministry," in *The Ministry and Mental Health*, Hans Hoffman, ed. (New York: Association Press, 1960), pp. 101-126.

[15] Allen Wheelis, *The Quest for Identity* (New York: Norton and Co., Inc., College Edition, 1958), pp. 19-20.

ready unsteady on their feet, who might once have found the churches a kind of scaffolding, are now ever more likely to fall.

This is why the denominations increasingly try to offer what support and help they can to today's troubled man of the cloth. One such place is the Northeast Career Center at Princeton, New Jersey, organized by Rev. Edward S. Golden. The clients are mostly Presbyterian. Golden says, "There seems to be in many of our religious traditions a real though subtle contempt for ourselves as persons and psychological beings. The characteristic trait of ministers is low self-esteem. I find the same troubles among Catholics and Jews."

"When skills become obsolete," Dr. Harry Levinson, Director of the Division of Industrial Mental Health, told a religious conference, "they not only lose their meaning as instruments of economic security but also as instruments of *psychological* security, because a man then loses an important method of mastering some part of his world. . . . The pastor very often is in the position of going from church to church, hoping that each will be better than the last. He is doomed to a certain kind of frustration about this, experiencing each one, in so many instances, as a frustrating failure. . . . Many of today's pastors, I am afraid—and you know this better than I—have become a kind of ecclesiastical flotsam, floating from one church to another, seeking a shore to be washed upon where one can then for once relax and never have to worry. Little wonder then that we talk about increasing conflict, increasing stress, and increasing illness."

Still another specialist in clerical conflict is Knox Kreutzer, who describes himself as a "maverick" Episcopal priest. Kreutzer was a psychiatric consultant to the bishops of three Episcopal dioceses and runs a clinical center for ministers in Washington, D. C. "Sure," he says, "the bishops are aware of the problems, but have a few drinks with them and they tell you, 'Honestly, what can we do?' I see a sort of ministerial syndrome. The relation with father never came off. Papa was weak. Mother was strong. She approved the ministry as a choice, though Papa didn't. The son is a fugitive from the hurly-burly world, in search of himself. These themes conform to the religious symbols which are out of family life. There is God (the church), the Holy Ghost (the weak father) and the Virgin Mary (the strong mother). The guy going into the ministry comes with the desire to be reunited with the (strong) father, God. He marches out of seminary singing Te Deum but he is really looking for every symbol he can find to confirm his neurosis.

"There might be a valid reason for joining the ministry. There are still people who turn to the minister for help and he has a desire to help them. By and large, though, the churches are a home for those who are fugitives from the alarming changes taking place in society. The churches have been given a function as a sort of social maintenance man."

The idea of childlike dependency among ministers is also expressed by Daniel D. Walker, in *The Human Problems of the Minister:*

> We come now to the obvious but often neglected truth that, in relation to God, the minister should play the role of the child. There is that within each of us which demands the experience of sonship if we are to be happy. We must bow to something; we must have an authority; there must be an authority; there must be an ideal to look up to, a commander to listen to. Without this experience, something in us remains unfulfilled and we feel disinherited.[16]

The same theme is expressed in a different way by Margaretta K. Bowers, a psychiatrist who works frequently with clergymen. To her, "Many patients have gone into the ministry in search of love; never having experienced enough human love, they hope to find love in God."[17] She is concerned with the extent of homosexual impulses among ministers as an expression of this unfulfilled love-need. Homosexuality, she says, "is a problem that one

---

[16] Daniel D. Walker, *The Human Problems of the Minister* (New York: Harper & Bros., 1960), p. 129.
[17] Margaretta K. Bowers, *op. cit.*, p. 45.

does not talk about. More than half my male clergy population has suffered this crippling behavior symptom." The Protestant tradition, she maintains, "permits and encourages a man in his anger toward women." And she wonders, "Does Christianity actively promote the development of homosexuality and does the church give the homosexual a place in which he can hope to sublimate his homosexuality?"[18]

"There is a great deal of homosexuality in the ministry," maintains a Lutheran pastor, Ralph Peterson, former executive director of the Department of Ministry, Vocation and Pastoral Services at NCC. "It's tied up with their identity crises—who are they? they ask, and they don't know. It is one of the built-in hazards of the ministry. The passive-dependent, by definition, is seeking to resolve an identity crisis and might drift naturally into religion. So many ministers have magical expectation, as though the ministry will confer on you a certain humanity you are unable to have yourself."

It appears a valid conclusion that the great amount of denomination-hopping among American clergymen—60 per cent of the Episcopal clergy, for instance, come from other denominations—also reflects the minister's desire to find himself. When a clergyman says, as one told me, "I'd rather switch than fight," he may be expressing his psychological as well as theological needs. For although many similar themes run through American religion, there are also marked differences in denominational personalities. "I see at least three distinct denominational characteristics which I'd describe negatively," says Rev. Golden, "—the Southern Baptists, alienated, individualistic, aggressive, thick-skinned, narrow minded; the Episcopalians and Lutherans, passive-dependent, liturgical, effeminate; and the Presbyterians, who are somewhere in between."

Such differences can be expressed in many ways. To C. F. Middlefort, a Lutheran psychiatrist who heads the Committee on Basic Ideas Underlying Religion and Health of the NCC, "If one

[18] *Ibid.*, p. 12.

looks at psychopathology as expressing rebellion against the predominant theology of a denomination, one finds the difficulty in Lutherans concerns dogma and among Episcopalians social and communal life. These differences are reflected in the attitudes in the two denominations toward grace and in the involvement that patients develop intellectually and socially. The Lutherans overemphasize special grace and the Episcopalians common grace. The Lutherans with their lack of trust and their sense of guilt rebel against the authority of the penitential system. The Episcopalians with their reliance upon the community take it out on the social structure of the Church and society in their rebellion."

Lutheran pastors and members of their families, he points out, who were patients, "overemphasize authority at the expense of love and humanity," and rebellions to this family structure can take the form of paranoia. Calvinists, encouraged to devotion to duty, righteousness, and obedience, overloaded themselves with work and felt resentful, discouraged, and guilty. Methodist minister patients displayed social inferiority and hysterical symptoms. They had a great need to be busy and were dominated by women. The most violent "solutions" came from Pentecostal and Adventist patients—hysteria, attempts at suicide.

A Southern Baptist hospital in North Carolina has even indentified a "ministerial syndrome." The minister has spent all year repressing hostility and doing good for everybody and works even harder as his vacation nears. Secretly, though, he doesn't believe in vacations and having fun, and as the time approaches his hands begin to shake and he can't sleep. Bags packed, he heads out the driveway and then, his anxieties suddenly in full bloom, he heads for the hospital.

In the American mythology rural people from stable and religious backgrounds are supposed to be the best adjusted, but a study of ministers, missionaries and postulants who had come for psychiatric help did not substantiate the idea. Their mothers appeared often to be domineering, unconsciously seductive, provocative and rejecting, while the fathers were passive, hostile, withdrawn and dependent. "For these people, the relationship within the church tended to compensate in part for the deprivation they experienced within the family. In a very real sense, they could believe they were 'somebody' in terms of their religious beliefs and practices." This author thought, in the case of some, "it was tempting to relate their gastric ulcers to their missionary work."[19]

The fundamentalist preachers thought they had a direct and special relationship with God which sometimes resulted in hallucinatory experiences. "George," a young seminarian, had been moody and depressed, but after hearing an Evangelist preacher talk about sin, the church music roared in his ears. "I felt confused—sort of dazed. How can I describe those feelings? I reached up, but I was also in the depths. There was something I needed, but couldn't find, I thought. I left the meeting and walked and walked. My thoughts seemed unusually clear, yet they were confusing. I was tired so I sat on a bench in the park. A man asked me for a light; I didn't have one. Then it came to me with a flash. He was the agent of God. He'd asked for something I couldn't give. It was all clear to me now. There was meaning for me. I was to prepare so that when called I could give. I felt a sense of relief—of oneness."

For such people religious belief is a protective shell and if the belief is removed the ego collapses with it. Although this is putting the problem in an extreme form, the psychiatric consultants to ministers believe that the malaise is prevalent throughout organized religion. And the cure for the weak religious ego is thought to be some meaningful function, some identifiable usefulness for the clergyman. As one pastoral counselor told me, "The minister's role problem is not solved by advice but by his becoming a specialist."

And here is a central irony for religion. The term "pastoral counseling" is now common coin for the churches, and it has two sides. One side is the counseling *by* the clergyman, and the other

[19] C. W. Christensen, "The Occurrence of Mental Illness in the Ministry," *Journal of Pastoral Care*, 14 (1960), 143-49. Also, 17 (1963), 1-10.

of him. But just as the minister is reluctant to seek professional help, because he fears it will affect his career, and because a minister is supposed to be "spiritual" and immune from psychiatric woes, so the minister has distinct limitations as a counselor for others. For the moral beliefs of religion—built into its very structure—stop him from generating the full range of understanding and permissiveness that troubled people want when they come for help. He is, say the psychiatrists, unable to trust people. He is, in short, too close to, and too much like, his own parishioner.

Chapter Six

The People,
the Opiate of Religion

WHETHER it was in piety or riches, obedience or inspired revolt, hard work or gratuitous generosity, the great religions have usually taught that religious belief wrought changes in the human spirit. Worship of a Supreme Being ennobled, and religion inspired good people and better lives. However subtly, then, the Creator did manifest Himself in the faithful, His chosen people, who were, or should have been, qualitatively a little different from non-believers. Indeed the indications are that church members *are* different from the unchurched, but in ways that may well trouble the minister as he gazes down at his flock on a Sunday morning.

Obviously it's difficult to generalize about so many people from so many backgrounds and faiths, but among church leaders the suspicion is growing, backed up by studies often undertaken by the denominations themselves, that churches attract some kinds of people more than others. That these people may be more prejudiced, dependent, authoritarian, passive and resistant to change than ordinary citizens is a truly terrifying thought for those ecclesiastical philosophers who believe that the only hope for the survival of organized religion is to be ahead of, not behind, the general society. Actually, for many pastors the reverse of Karl Marx's famous formulation is true: The people are the opiate of religion.

There are about 320,000 churches in the U.S.—one for roughly every six hundred people, although not every community has one. Why do people join and sometimes attend? The reasons, naturally, vary. One Southerner sees church as "a filling station. We come in and gas up pretty often and you know it is a problem when you run out of gas. If you don't get in and get gassed up pretty often, you get in trouble." Some feel sanctified, while others find in religion comfort or aesthetic delight; and there are those who want to be seen and make connections, not always with the Almighty. Americans, too, appear to have an insurance mentality—let's join a church *just in case* there's a heaven and/or hell. It might be noted that at a supper for new members, forty-seven Presbyterians were asked why they joined the church. The answers varied, but not a single one mentioned a belief in or the call of a deity of any kind.

Surely it's no news that the most frequent reason given for becoming church members—substantiated by many observers—is "for the children." (This is why the precipitous drop in Sunday School attendance is an ominous portent for organized religion.) For William H. Whyte, in *The Organization Man*, "new suburbanites customarily approach the church through their children." Plumbing the churchy motivations of "upward-mobile," college-educated Congregationalists in the Hartford, Connecticut, area, two researchers, Dennison Nash and Peter Berger, also discovered children to be the church key. "My daughter started in Sunday School. I decided that as long as we were bringing up the children in the church we ought to join." "It rounds out their education." "When I joined the church I said that it was hypocritical on my part. . . . I don't feel quite as clean as I did before—to be honest with you—because I didn't do it for me—I mean trying to do something for someone else that I should have done for my own feelings, for my own reasons."

Commenting on answers like these, the authors concluded, ruefully, "Most of the people see nothing wrong with superficial or even hypocritical involvement with organized religion, if it is conceived to benefit the children." Church membership, it seems, is often a modern version of "And a little child shall lead them."

Some church leaders challenge the logic of exposing a child to a religion the parent holds shakily in order to give the child "free choice" about his future religion, or the lack of it. The churches, increasingly, want committed people, not an endless chain of non-believers or semi-believers foisting off religion on their children, who foist it off on theirs, resembling what Eric Berne might term a "Game Called Church." The superficiality of the typical church attachment has made ecclesiastical officials wonder about the wisdom of the tremendous membership drives that occurred after World War II, culminating in the "religious revival" of the 1950's, which brought into the fold a great many members on whom the churches can count for neither loyalty, theological education or financial support. "In the nineteenth century," says Bishop Corrigan, "there was a general revulsion to Christianity and we never did get very committed to it. We've had illusions of very great success from time to time but only because people began to look at religion as a status symbol."

Religion has been called a "paradoxical sociological-theological duality," and, at least on the surface, it is a house of many contradictions. Let us examine a few of them: Religious leaders today stress experimentation, worldliness, and being up-to-date, but the response of the parishioners, typically, is nostalgia. "Do I sound," asks a writer in *Fortune*, expressing bewilderment at the new ideas, "like someone looking back to the religion of divine revelation that the old horse used to haul me off to listen to? It could be true—an unashamed admission."

Faced on the one side with traditional, nostalgic, even pastoral expectations of the parishioners—whose disillusionment would result in mass defections and even a church collapse—and on the other by the demands of a small but highly vocal and important minority demanding radical change—whose defection would deprive the churches of their liveliest sparks—those in the churchly hierarchy have to perform what R. H. Edwin Espy, General Secretary of the NCC, calls "a balancing act." Nonetheless, the church leadership, despite the pressures to keep traditional religion immaculate, cautiously at times and outspokenly at others, has consistently staked out positions which are more liberal than its parishioners'. This has created the Janus head of American religion, with its leaders and intellectuals saying one thing while the bulk of the believers think and do quite another.

Consider, for instance, the 1967 statement of the Presbyterian Church in the U.S.A. that peace should be sought "even at the expense of national security." It is difficult to believe that the ordinary Presbyterian churchgoer could subscribe to such a plank. Many church leaders, Protestant, Jewish and Catholic, including the Pope, have expressed misgivings or outright hostility to the American involvement in Vietnam without noticeably budging the consensus in a church-filled nation. The Catholic diocese of Chicago has taken forthright stands on integration, but it was in predominantly Catholic districts where freedom marchers, including priests and nuns, were stoned. Says Matthew Ahmen, of the National Catholic Conference for Interracial Justice, "If you put the integration question to the Chicago diocese it would lose."

As early as 1947 the established church of the South, the Southern Baptist, made a strong official statement on race, repeated in 1966. The church (or convention, as it's called) should, it said, "recognize its responsibility for the promotion of interracial good-will and urge upon our Baptist people and all Christians the duty of ordering our racial attitudes and actions in accordance with Christian truth and Christian love." There is a Baptist church in Charleston, S. C., with a plaque honoring "a leader in civil rights," but these were rights wrested from the national Episcopal Church in the nineteenth century, and despite the exhortations, the Baptist Church gives few indications of continuing the civil rights tradition into the twentieth. To this day Southern Baptist Sunday School literature never shows pictures of Negroes and whites together and the word "integration" is rarely used.

Just how far, in fact, the Southern Baptists will go in support of their own version of "Christian truth and Christian love" was displayed by a church in the Kirkwood section of Atlanta, Ga. In 1966 the church sold its buildings and property, which had cost over one million dollars, for $300,000 because Negroes were coming into the neighborhood. It was publicly congratulated by a Southern Baptist minister for "integrity" because it paid off its debts! ("Our job," says a Southern Baptist spokesman, off the record, "is to speak to the church *without losing members.*")

"It isn't that our people hate Negroes," I was assured by a high-ranking official of the largely Southern-based U.S. Presbyterian Church. "It's just that they can't *stand* change." I found virtual unanimity in the views of newspaper editors and other local observers, not just in the South but in the North as well, that ministers are frequently constrained on race and a broad range of social issues by their parishioners. All but nine of the 35 Mississippi Methodist ministers who signed a statement for racial justice lost their jobs, and such firings are by no means confined to the South. Studies have shown that there is a definite migration of ministers to areas where the mental climate is comfortable—northern segregationist ministers moving south, southern integrationist ministers going north, creating in segregationist situations the sort of unanimity that occurred in Little Rock in 1957, when "generally the ministers tacitly consented to a public dissociation of moral criteria from the issue of segregation versus integration, to the extent that, contrary to the positions taken by the national and regional bodies of all church groups, the loudest voices applying religious and moral criteria to this issue were those crying that integration violates the will of God. For most of the others, the religious and moral dimensions seemed simply not to be relevant."[1]

The churchgoer might choose to reply that he has his own standards of relevance, and liberal social ideas aren't among them. The question then arises, what *is* relevant and meaningful about religion? The Bible? Theology? For Rabbi Max J. Routenberg, president of the Rabbinical Assembly, the rabbi's skill and competence "are being tested now as never before because his people are virtually denuded of all Jewish practice and innocent of all Jewish knowledge." In a period of rocketing Bible sales, 53 per cent of Americans could not name even one of the first four books of the Old Testament. Among one large group of Christians, 98 per cent of whom had Bibles in their homes, 30 per cent didn't know that the Ten Commandments are in the Old Testament, 40 per cent couldn't place the Lord's Prayer in the New Testament with certainty, and of the 80 per cent who could start the Lord's Prayer more than half couldn't finish it. "Service to others" is a basic component of the Christian faith, but in survey after survey, "helping other people," like nice guys, always finishes last in the list of things members connect with church. Indeed, 80 per cent of church members have reported themselves more concerned with a comfortable life than the hereafter, and more than half have admitted that religious beliefs have no effect on the way they conduct themselves outside of church.

There is evidence, too, that for many people the faith itself is skin-deep and fragile. Take death, with whose rhythms the churches resound. At the University of Chicago's Billings Hospital the chaplain, teamed with psychiatrists, interviewed terminally ill

[1] Ernest Q. Campbell and Thomas F. Pettigrew, *Christians in Racial Crisis —A Study of Little Rock's Ministry* (Washington, D. C.: Public Affairs Press, 1959), p. 40.

patients to see how much help religion was. The chaplain asked the patients to talk about what was happening to them, how they felt, and what could be done, in their last moments, to give their lives "meaning." Those who used religion as a crutch were more fearful of dying than those who had genuine belief. "I would say that one-half of people who professed faith in organized religion turn out, in terminal illness, to have only a quasi-religious faith," said the chaplain, Rev. Carl Nighswonger. "Those with solid faith die more peacefully, but no more so than people without religious faith who have come to terms with death. It is a chilling thought for those who live with the idea of Christian exclusiveness, but agnostics and atheists may die just as peacefully as believers, if they have been able to accept death as part of life."

In trying to explain such seeming discrepancies between the ideals and actualities of organized religion one could merely say that there are "good" and "not-so-good" believers and let it go at that. But there is a theory which seems to bind together the contradictions of organized religion into a concrete whole, albeit more of a sociological than theological one. It is explained by Gerhard Lenski in The Religious Factor: "Basically," he says, "our theory leads us to think of contemporary American religious groups not only as associations, but as subcommunities as well; not merely as the carriers of religious norms in any narrow sense, but as the carriers of complex subcultures relevant to almost all phases of human existence. Also, our theory leads us to see these religiously based subcultures not merely as the products of present environmental influences, but equally as the products of the social heritage of the group—which . . . involves the influence of both former environments and former personnel."[2]

The idea, then, is that the religious subcommunities exist somewhat apart from the formal churches. They may justify themselves in the name of religion, and use the church as headquarters, but they are not identical with the church itself. This view gives us a

[2] Gerhard Lenski, The Religious Factor (Garden City, N.Y.: Doubleday and Company, Inc., Anchor Books Edition, 1963), p. 344.

way to account for why people can be "religious," church members in good standing, and yet get small comfort from their faith at death; why blatantly anti-biblical actions can be construed as Christian, since they are really the mores of the Christian sub-community, or why church attendance, at least in some faiths, can be interpreted so casually—because it is really the group that matters, not the observance.

Consider the Jews. Only a small per cent of Jews go to synagogue with any regularity, yet the Jewish *centers*, which have been identified as "purposeless ghettoism," thrive in the U.S. The rationale for these costly suburban kibbutzim was that they provided necessary social and welfare services which would be otherwise unavailable, but as community facilities of all kinds have enormously increased, as Jews themselves have come to occupy a highly favorable economic position, the centers must continue to exist for a different reason—that of keeping Jews together as a group. The idea is made explicit by one of the fathers of the Jewish center idea, Rabbi Mordecai M. Kaplan. "It therefore seemed to me that the only way to counteract the disintegrating influences within as well as without Jewish life was to create the conditions that would not only set in motion socially and psychologically constructive forces, but would also make them forces for religion. What was needed . . . was to transform the synagogue into a . . . neighborhood Jewish center. Instead of the primary purpose of congregational organization being worship, it should be social togetherness."[3]

McCall's Magazine religion is, then, the shining light. Its social togetherness side is greatly elaborated as safe; "nice" forms of expression are substituted for "dangerous" or "worldly" ones. An extreme example of this is the Southern Baptist who accused me of being "worldly" because I drove a convertible down South. Unworldly Baptist ladies, to this very day, must use cardholders for playing cards because they are unaccustomed to the slippery

[3] Quoted in Marshall Sklare, *Conservative Judaism—An American Religious Movement* (Glencoe, Ill.: Free Press, 1955), pp. 135-36.

pasteboards. The game they play is called Rook, with the suits numbered from one to thirteen—to avoid wicked face cards—and designated by color. Ordinary or "gambling" cards are "worldly."

But with some exceptions—the pacifist Quakers, for instance— the religious groups do not operate outside of the safe circumfer- ence of American beliefs, despite some minor taboos. They are thus at the mercy of the secular winds. The prominent Protestant writer, Martin E. Marty, could have been speaking of Protestants or Jews when he said that "Catholic parishes are in trouble, deep trouble. . . . Their attitudes are [often] shaped by their political allegiances, economic class, social commitments, by their kinds of employment, and by the mass media of communications." They may cheer their own—Baptists in the space program, Lutheran beauty queens or "Anthony Celebreze, Seventeenth Catholic in the Cabinet," the Fellowship of Christian Athletes, or the Catholic Mother of the Year—but they have singularly failed to come up with an individual perspective. So one expects to read in the reli- gious magazines, and does, arguments as to whether a tavern keeper should have been elected to the church council, or, mar- velously: "The women of St. John's Church voted to fight against the sale of pornographic publications at their May meeting."

The Catholicism the church modernists will have difficulty changing is the sort revealed in the diocesan papers, such as: "The Mass that day and the office for priests and Religious will specifi- cally honor Blessed John Neumann [a Redemptorist priest- immigrant]. Establishment of the feast also means that statues and pictures of Blessed Neumann now may be placed in churches here [Pittsburgh] for proper veneration. Also, pious devotions such as novenas will be permitted if approval is obtained from the bishop."

"In this period of turbulence I can count basically on the loy- alty of two groups," says Pittsburgh's Bishop John Wright, "the conservatives and the ethnic subpopulation, neither of whom has heard of Teilhard de Chardin."

Listen one Saturday or Sunday to a sermon of a typical rabbi or minister. The theme is all too likely to be a question to which everyone knows the answer in advance: "Is God dead?" (No.) "Are the young without morality?" (This topic—the answer to which is also no—never fails to interest the predominantly older churchgoers.) "Is there hope for mankind?" "Can we live without God?" Such interrogatives are followed by a series of quotes pasted together, without a hint of discipline, from whatever sources happened to land on the minister's desk that week—an editorial or a news event, a scientific article, a line or two of poetry—followed by a biblical quote and the predictable conclusion. There is a complete and conspicuous absence of any *religious* insight. "I try," one minister told me, "to give them a little of this and a little of that, a little uplift, a little scaring, a little food for thought."

The bland diet served up by the ministers may provide a certain nourishment, however. It gives sanction for one's life, reassurance that though one may feel powerless one is still "at the center" where the power—that is, reality—ultimately is, and a refuge against suffering, real or imagined. (Mingled here may be a kind of leftover defensiveness from the days when many religious groups, preëminently Jews and Catholics but also many others, were actively discriminated against.) Essentially, as church leaders have recognized, this frame of mind is dependent, and alert pastors sometimes deplore parishioners' dependency on them. When the minister loves them, God does too. If they have troubles these are signs of God's anger, and the acceptance and understanding of the minister means that God loves them once more. "The come-alive people aren't here," says a New York minister. "By and large it's the bruised and wounded who come to church."

These themes—wistfulness, dependency, sadness—are also sounded clearly in the hymnals: "Help me sing on when my heart breaks in sadness . . ." "Ho-ly Ghost, with pow'r divine, Cleanse this guilt-y heart of mine . . ." "I need Jesus, my need I now confess; No friend like him in times of deep distress. . . ." Or, "No One Ever Cared for Me like Jesus":

I would love to tell you what I think of Jesus
Since I found in Him a friend so strong and true;
I would tell you how He changed my life completely.
He did something that no oth-er friend could do.

No one ever cared for me like Je-sus,
There's no oth-er friend so kind as He;
No one else could take the sin and darkness from me,
O how much He cared for me.

"For a century or more," writes a Congregationalist minister, "our hymns have continued to feed upon themselves, sopping up second-rate music and poetry from the secular world's leavings and hallowing it with mindless piety and tasteless sentimentality." It is, he says, a world of the imagination populated with devils, demons and witches and "a whole panoply of superstitions about the virginity of Jesus' mother, the miraculous powers of his 'sacred heart' and the like." But it is also a picture of a lonely people banded together, heads lifted in hopeful song. And if Jesus cares and Jesus saves, it is *me* and *my* salvation that he cares for.

A good case is the South, home of what is seen there as religious individualism. Students of Southern religion, like the Rev. Samuel Southard, believe that what is displayed is in reality quite the reverse. "Dependence is the dominant theme of Southern religion," he says. "The beliefs, morals and manners of Southerners have been based on or attributed to an authority beyond self. This feeling of dependence has been so pervasive that conservative Protestantism or evangelical piety is usually presented as a major characteristic of the region." For Southard, there ought to be, indeed, absolute dependence on God but only relative dependence on one's culture and fellow men, including the minister; and not just down South but rather pervasively in the U.S. church members confuse the two.

This concentration on the religious *me* and *my* religious subcommunity, to whose ideas are attributed divine authority and to which the religious person reacts dependently, is reflected in many ways by the church set-up. Frequently, for instance, churches are too small to be self-supporting. "A lot of churches should close up shop," says Truman Douglass, a ranking official of the United Church of Christ. But in churches where the membership decide such matters for themselves, the leaders can beseech and beseech, without results. Ecclesiasts generally think that the country is rampantly overchurched, with a tremendous excess capacity of pews, because each little congregation insists on having its own building and Hammond organ and refuses to worship with its neighbors. Protestant churches usually figure that it takes two hundred and fifty to four hundred members to make a church self-supporting. Churches with a poorer constituency, which contributes less, need more members than rich churches to become financially independent—but in most denominations by far the largest number of churches are those with comparatively few parishioners. (The Catholics are an exception to this rule. Their churches arc larger and used more, and one reason for Catholic strength in the U.S. is simple efficiency.) This means that the church membership often cannot pay adequate salaries to ministers, and this, in turn, is related to the lowered quality of applicants to the profession. (Nor do a lot of ministers want to get stuck in some little outpost of Christianity with a handful of insularly minded parishioners.) It also means that many churches can give little or nothing to the denominations for their work in the world; in fact, they are a constant drain. In one of the richest American churches, the U.S. Presbyterian, whose average member gives twice what the average Methodist does, 16 per cent of the churches require denominational support to stay alive. The Catholics, too, fearful of losing loyal supporters, maintain costly, understrength ethnic parishes, though such parishes are scored by high Catholic spokesmen as "absurd."

One side effect of this organizational retentiveness of the smaller churches is to throw power and control to the richer churches which can afford to give money to the denominations, and which, having paid the piper, can call the religious tune.

"We walk an institutional tightrope here," I was told by an Episcopal diocesan official. "For us the central question is how to get money to operate. We wonder how much our behavior is determined by fear. We don't want to antagonize our financial base, which is a handful of rich, conservative churches who contribute more than half our income. As it is, a number of parishes cut their contributions because of our stand on civil rights."

To indicate what the diocese was confronted with, he showed me a classified church document which pointed out that the "central core of the church [is] likely to be composed of people who value the local church as (a) a conservator and sanctifier of their social and class values or (b) a club of like-minded people sponsoring satisfying leisure-time activities and projects. The clergy who try to modify this are faced with cancellations of pledges or an exodus of outraged people."

It might seem to a visiting Indian or Chinese something of a social luxury that congeries of like-minded, henotheistic, or ingroup-worshiping people—steeple climbers, if you will—could afford to maintain for a handful of members a house of worship and the full-time services of a pastor to look after their "spiritual needs." That these needs, not those of others, are paramount in the concerns of organized religion is shown by the way church dollars are really spent. Let us pause for a moment to look at the U.S. Presbyterians, whose income figures are fairly easy to round out.

The almost one million U.S. Presbyterians each give an average of $119.20 a year to their church. One of the highest giving rates, it is clearly not a substantial portion of the churchgoers' incomes, and it may be tax-deductible at that. Altogether U.S. Presbyterians contribute $112,000,000 to their churches, of which 85 per cent is retained by the local churches for running the parishes or in building funds. Very little of this 85 per cent is used for philanthropic or social purposes beyond the church walls. Most of the remaining 15 per cent is used for the administration of the denomination and for evangelism. At a time when churches want to show their muscle through helping to fight poverty and slums, the U.S. Presbyterians could afford one million dollars for "specialized ministries" which handle such projects. To the Church World Service for famine relief over the globe, the U.S. Presbyterians gave $218,000. (As we shall see, the principal supporter of church overseas charity is the U.S. Government.) For the National Council of Churches—the main action arm for Protestantism—the U.S. Presbyterians coughed up $212,000, or $.00139— less than a fifth of a cent—per member. The paucity of church giving is usually compared with how much Americans spend on cigarettes or whisky, but a more apt comparison, it would seem, is with candy bars.

The magnanimity of the U.S. Presbyterians is fully equalled by churches of the other denominations, none of whom, for all the bazaars and cake sales, seem to have anything left for the world when they have finished buying artificial flowers and installing electronic chimes. Thus in a recent year the large Presbyterian Church in the U.S.A could scrape up only one dollar per member for church world relief. The Episcopalians, with one of the better records, expend an estimated total of fifteen cents per member per year on all forms of social action. The Catholics, likewise, are said to give thirteen or fourteen cents per head for social action. The churches may cry out against the war in Vietnam, but the Presbyterians of the U.S.A. were able to find for a year's relief there only $46,000, the price of one not-too-large suburban house.

The churches will, however, give unstintingly for expensive modern denominational headquarters buildings, for glossy magazines, public relations men, statisticians, IBM and Xerox machines, endless travel for officials who scuttle constantly from conference to conference, and for high conclaves of churchmen wearing their name badges who may occupy entire hotels. All this effort and expense goes toward maintaining and, hopefully, enlarging the church organizations, and the focus is not out but in, toward self-nurture and self-interest.

The leadership of the churches cannot afford to upset these

established patterns of church giving and spending because to do so would be to run, head on, into the needs of the parishioners. What increasingly troubles many ecclesiastical intellectuals is that the mental makeup of churchgoers is not geared to the demands relevant religion wants to make on them. There is evidence that churchgoers make up a *population* with clearly discernible traits. As one informed student of churches puts it, "We talk about relevance and getting into the world, but do we have the proper characterology in the churches? The members are, in general, passive, pious, superstitious and socially isolated. How did we get them? My hope is that it was by selection and reinforcement. A more depressing possibility is that we created them."

Take a study by a Methodist sociologist named Leo Rippy, Jr., of young North Carolina Methodists. Comparing them with ordinary high school students, Rippy found the Methodists more "passive, withdrawn, compulsive, authoritarian, dependent." Now, Rippy says, an authoritarian person is highly dependent on those persons, ideals or ideas which he sees as having authority, and this relates to his inability to distinguish between information about the world and the sources of that information. Calling these closed, as opposed to open, people, Rippy described closed persons as those using the future tense more than the present, more anxious than open people about the future, suffering from more anxiety symptoms, intolerant of ambiguity and so on. Evidently concerned about the kind of people Methodists were turning out, Rippy asked, "Are these differences due to the effect of a particular church on its youth? Or are the differences due to the gathering of a particular kind of youth in a particular church?"[4]

---

[4] Unpublished paper presented at the meeting of the Religious Research Association in June, 1966. Rippy's study was based on the findings of Dr. Milton Rokeach in *The Open and Closed Mind* (New York: Basic Books, 1960). For Rokeach, "to say that a person is dogmatic or that his belief system is closed is to say something about the way he believes and the way he thinks—not only about single issues but also about networks of issues." He offers as a basic characteristic for defining whether a mind is open or closed "the extent to which a person can receive, evaluate, and act on relevant information received from the outside on its own intrinsic

Still lurking in the American ideal is the young man or woman, fastidious, high on endurance for such things as church lessons, big on his family, feeling full of rectitude and close to God. But according to such studies as Rippy's, which have been undertaken in several parts of the country, such models of good behavior also may display a low interest in the other sex, a denial of impulse, aggressiveness or hostility and a poor resistance to outside authority. It's a truism that not being able to let go reveals a stunted personality; it may not be so obvious that an inability to understand aggression in oneself leads to an inability to understand it in others. Christian hostility to hostility, some think, brings an emphasis on "dialogue" when action is needed. What was true of a Protestant group in San Diego might have reference to Catholic experience since Vatican II. The San Diego churchgoers were ready and willing to criticize the church, but only when given permission to do so.

That church members establish identity through the group, that this group is characteristically more illiberal in social attitudes than non-church-members, is so well established as to hardly need comment. "Two contrary sets of threads are woven into the fabric of all religion—the warp of brotherhood and the woof of bigotry," the famous sociologist Gordon Allport has said. "It is a well established fact that, on the average, churchgoers in our country harbor more racial, ethnic and religious prejudice than do non-churchgoers." "By and large," writes Gerhard Lenski, in italics, ". . . the religious subcommunities *foster and encourage a provincial and authoritarian view of the world.*" The observation has been backed up by many studies. "There seems to be no doubt that subjects who reject organized religion are less prejudiced on average than those who, in one way or another, accept it," wrote T. W. Adorno, as a result of massive surveys. Though he was able

---

merits, unencumbered by irrelevant factors in the situation arising within the person, or from the outside. By irrelevant external pressures we have in mind most particularly the pressures of reward and punishment arising from external authority figures."

to find little or no difference between Catholics and Protestants, regular or irregular church attenders, he found notably less ethnocentricity on the part of people who reject religion. Adorno related the "exploitative dependency" of religious people to American middle-class life, and he said, "Submission to and dependence upon parental authority is an important determinant of ethnocentrism. . . ." He went on: "Belonging to or identifying oneself with a religious body in America today does not mean that one thereby takes over the traditional Christian values of tolerance, brotherhood, and equality. On the contrary, it appears that those values are more firmly held by people who do not affiliate with any religious group. It may be that religious affiliation or church attendance is of little importance one way or another in determining social attitudes, that the great majority of middle-class Americans identify themselves with some religious denomination as a matter of course, without thinking much about it. . . . It may be argued, however, that this conventional approach to religion expresses through identification with the *status quo*, submission to external authority, and readiness to emphasize moralistically the difference between those who 'belong' and those who do not, to differentiate members of the large denominations from the non-religious. . . ."[5]

Almost two decades have passed since these words were written, but if American expectations of tolerance have risen sharply, church members have stayed the same. A five-year study by the Jewish organization B'nai B'rith showed that 60 per cent of church members still hold the Jews responsible for killing Christ, and another survey found that 80 per cent of church members held some "explicitly negative beliefs about Jews as a group. . . . Nearly half acknowledged they bore unfriendly feelings toward Jews because of those beliefs." Fewer than half of these Christians gave Jews the right to be admitted to vacation resorts, or would sympathize with a Jewish store owner called "a crook like all the

---

[5] T. W. Adorno, *et al.*, *The Authoritarian Personality* (New York: Harper and Bros., 1950), p. 219.

Jews." And only 5 per cent of Americans with anti-Semitic views were said to lack all rudiments of a religious basis.[6]

What, indeed, is the religious imperative to practice tolerance or equality, much less love, for 50 per cent of the Catholics, 55 per cent of the Baptists and 62 per cent of the Luthcrans who think that God is more concerned with attendance at church than He is with the treatment of men? What for the Southern Baptists, almost three times as many of whom think that cursing will keep God's chillun out of heaven as those who think anti-Semitism will?

On the basis of religious beliefs, the denominations have been separated into five major groups: the liberals—Congregationalists, Methodists and Episcopalians; the moderates—Disciples of Christ and Presbyterians; the conservatives—the American Lutherans and the American (or Northern) Baptists; the fundamentalists— the Missouri Synod Lutherans and the Southern Baptists; and the Catholics, who differ from the conservatives only on the question of Papal Infallibility. The ordering was established on the basis of responses like "I know God really exists and I have no doubt about it," "Jesus was born of a virgin," "Jesus walked on water," "Miracles actually happened just as the Bible says they did." Fundamentalists, as might be expected, answered such questions in the affirmative more consistently than conservatives did, and so on up the line. And the liberals displayed a higher degree of tolerance and open-mindedness toward others than the conservatives and fundamentalists.[7] This is not surprising, since social and theological conservatism have long been known as soul mates. Now let's see how the most liberal church members feel.

The United Church of Christ conducted a study of its membership's willingness to accept those of other racial or ethnic background, or what it called "social distance." Seven out of ten of

[6] Charles Y. Glock and Rodney Stark, *Christian Belief and Anti-Semitism* (New York: Harper & Row, 1966), p. 160.

[7] Charles Y. Glock and Rodney Stark, *Religion and Society in Tension* (Chicago: Rand McNally, 1965), pp. 91, 121ff.

those surveyed were white-collar workers, managerial, professional or technological people—in short, the WASP upper middle class. Neither education, income or church attendance made a difference in outlook, however. What did were age, length of church membership and commitment to traditional religious belief. The majority believed that the traditional statements about virgin birth, revelation, the resurrection of Jesus Christ are true. They believed in immortality, equality before God, and in the Bible as the Word of God, but they did not accept the equally traditional ideas of original sin and hell. They showed a strong belief in personal morality and gave high priority to the expectation that church helps "to build a good moral foundation for my personal life."

So far so good, from the church liberal's point of view. But while 86 per cent believed that "all men are equal in the eyes of God," less than half would give the denomination the right to issue policy statements in such matters. And, if action means more than words, the record would be somewhat worse, for less than one Congregationalist white in ten would admit Negroes "to close kinship by marriage" and only three in eight would admit them into their "clubs as chums." Only a third of the metropolitan area population favored non-discriminatory housing laws, and about the same percentage would admit Negroes to live on their streets as neighbors.

It must not be assumed that the WASP churchgoers exclude only Negroes, for they evidently wish to keep others at a sanitary distance, too. Only 30 per cent would admit Jews to close kinship by marriage, only 60 per cent to their clubs. Twenty-two per cent would not even admit Jews to *citizenship*. And the Jews, in these eyes, are obviously more acceptable than Orientals, Indians and other non-whites.

By contrast, and in contradistinction to an opinion widely held, Negroes in this study emerged significantly more open to others than whites. "The suggestion," said the authors, "that Negroes tend to be anti-Semitic found no factual basis in our data." For the liberal leadership of the United Church of Christ, the conclusion could not have made pleasant reading. "Thus," the report said, between denominational expectations and the white parishioners attitudes, "there seems to be a gap. . . ." The report asked plaintively, ". . . what must the church do to move its parishioners into the world so that the Christian can become more responsive to its needs?"[8]

The answer may well be "nothing." One study puts those who do not use religion instrumentally—that is, for other than reinforcement of their own ends—as low as 10 per cent of the membership. The vast majority, dependent on group authority, identifying the universe of the sacred with themselves, showing a strong distaste for and superiority to other races (in a world in which the white race is increasingly outnumbered), fearing formlessness and lack of order (in a world which won't satisfy them), doesn't seem to be the right material for the kind of Christian soldiers the reformers have in mind. For Max Weber, the German sociologist who wrote some of the archetypical works on religion, there is always a tension between religion's ideal goals and the possibilities of attaining them on earth. This tension, he says, can be resolved in two ways: one is through escape from conflict and a concentration on the other-worldly, the course church membership has chosen. The other is to try to bring the world into line with the aims of religion, in short, to act. But since the churches, in this respect, cannot rely on the faithful, since there is a strong and active need for church organizations to prove that religion is a social institution, they have been compelled to go to Caesar for help.

[8] Yoshio Fukiyama, *The Parishioners; A Sociological Interpretation* (Abstract) (New York: United Church Board for Homeland Ministries, United Church of Christ), April 22, 1966.

Chapter Seven

In the State We Trust

As the whole world knows—for surely we have trumpeted it enough—in America the church and state are separate. "Congress shall make no laws respecting an establishment of religion," thunders the First Amendment, and as a result the government Shalt Not levy taxes in support of religion, participate in the affairs of religious organizations, force a person to go (or not to go) to church or punish him for "entertaining" religious beliefs (or disbeliefs). The settlement of the church-state conflict is considered by scholars as one of the great decisions shaping modern political systems, while the secular commandment to keep the church and the state separate is drilled into schoolboys across the land and, at least in public, revered by politicians and churchmen who wouldn't dream of being guilty of what used to be, anyway, the longest word in the English language, antidisestablishmentarianism.

The evidence is, though, that church and state, far from keeping a Jeffersonian "wall" between them, have developed a remarkably cuddlesome relationship, especially in recent years, to the point where "In the State We Trust" might well be organized religion's motto. Indeed, such is the support proffered the churches by the state that one can reasonably wonder whether organized religion could survive in America in anything resembling its present form without the government's strong arm to lean upon. Ironically, perhaps, it is precisely in those arenas in which the churches seek to justify themselves by involvement in the world that this assistance is most urgently requested.

At least in theory, the "state" means the public, churched and unchurched, free thinkers, atheists, agnostics, secularists, church-haters and church-lovers alike. If it could be shown that all, or almost all, Americans were believers in or supporters of organized religion, then government aid might be construed as voluntary community efforts which do not violate the church-state wall, and this may be a reason why the exaggerated picture of a churchy America, as portrayed by the misleading religious statistics, has gone unchallenged so long. The state, for its part, evidently hopes to gain from organized religion a measure of social stability and unity for American policy in the Cold War. The community likes religion, too, not only because the local pillars are usually associated with the churches but as part of its longing for a safe society, its benign pseudo-recollection of a "golden age" without violence and racial strife. Thus, although it's clear that a substantial portion of the population is not connected with organized religion, that large numbers of others have only the most superficial association with it, that a lip-service belief in God as registered by

95 per cent of the population cannot be twisted into a vote for *churches*, everybody is required to support them, like it or not.

The complex story of government aid to religion begins at the local level, where the community shows itself four-square behind the churches by offering them free police and fire protection. In cities, a yellow stripe on the curb before the churches often designates an area of permanent no-parking. The desperate motorist circling the block may well wonder how many funerals and weddings take place at night or why the clergyman's car, by virtue of the ticket-exempt DD on the license plate, should be very nearly divine as far as the parking laws are concerned.

But the principal gift conferred on the churches by the localities —a tradition begun by Constantine in an effort to make Christianity the official religion of the Roman Empire—is, of course, exemptions from local property taxes. In New York City, where I live, the Guild of St. Ives, a group of Episcopal lawyers, puts the value of property used for religious purposes at $700 million, and it says taxes on this property would yield $30 million a year. For a city the size of New York, with a budget of five billion dollars, this is not an overwhelming amount, but neither is it the whole picture. For the revenue is based on the appraised valuation of the land and buildings, which may be low. If commercial structures were built on the same land instead, the tax revenue would be much higher. From the churches' point of view, $30 million would be an exceedingly large amount if they were asked to pay it. And the exemptions permit the denominations to cling, perhaps in the hope of another religious revival, to large downtown churches with handfuls of parishioners—property which might otherwise be yielding taxes that might be used to fight religion's present chief enemy, poverty in the inner city.

"It's not politic to talk about taxing the churches," a high official of the New York City Tax Commission told me. Still, there is a pressure from the outside to do so. The Women's City Club of New York believes that "the present State policy of full exemption from real estate taxes for properties of charitable, religious, and educational organizations must be re-evaluated in the light of the great growth of such exempt properties." It points out that such exemptions began in colonial times and rested on the theory that non-profit institutions contributed to the general welfare by offering services the government would otherwise have to render. But most of the welfare services offered by churches have been taken over by the state, and religion ministers principally to the needs of its own in-groups. Aware of this, some religious people, like the Guild of St. Ives, have advocated that churches pay property taxes, either in full or on all the property except that used for the services, and over the U.S. a few churches have voluntarily given money to their communities in lieu of taxes—not the full amount, however. Generally, though, on the question of exemptions the churches have stood pat.

Throughout the U.S. the story is the same. Rhode Island, an official there estimates, loses $10 million a year from deductions offered to religious and educational institutions. (A good deal of property listed as "educational" is really church-connected, as with denominational colleges and parochial schools.) One study concludes, "In many typically large cities, such church or church-related property now totals 10 per cent of all real estate, 25 per cent or more of the exempt portion, and from 50 to 70 per cent of the exempt portion that is privately owned."[1]

The author uses as his model four "representative" U.S. cities —Buffalo, the District of Columbia, Baltimore and Denver. In Washington, the true valuation of church and church-related property, excluding church-owned business properties, was more than $600 million in 1964, in Baltimore, $300 million, and so on, to which must be added what inflation has done to such valuations since. The total of Catholic exemptions is higher than the Protestant, but this is because of their parochial schools, while Protes-

---

[1] Martin A. Larson, *Church Wealth and Business Income* (New York: Philosophical Library, 1965), p. 59. Larson's book is almost completely unsung, perhaps because he indicates a rather doctrinaire anti-Catholic bias— *i.e.*, phrases like "under the control of the Vatican" when referring to Roman Catholic property. But there is no reason to think his findings inaccurate.

tants tend to concentrate their holdings in churches. All in all, on the basis of the four pilot cities, the assessed valuation of religious property in the U.S. was said to be $32 billion in 1964, with a cash value of $80 billion, and the taxes on Catholic property alone, were it assessed like other property, would yield one billion dollars a year. Another estimate says that church property-tax exemptions deprive the government of $16 billion a year in revenue.

Whatever the amount, the exemptions for churches—mostly white, middle-class churches—is evidently considerable, representing tax dollars which must be found somewhere else, from sales taxes and the like. The actual budget of the local churches is usually furnished by contributions, and here, too, the government gives a helping hand. The National Bureau of Economic Research has estimated that in 1960 private giving to religious organizations, including a small amount of endowments but excluding parochial schools, came to $4.5 billion a year. For individuals there is, of course, a standard charitable tax deduction, but for those who use the long tax form much greater deductions are possible. "The deductibility of charitable contributions within the framework of the progressive tax system makes philanthropy increasingly less painful for individuals as they move up the ladder of the rate structure," says one expert. The rich member of a local church can very nearly have it both ways. He scores, presumably, points in heaven for his generosity, which may have cost him little because his contributions are deductible from taxes. Further, in giving wealthy contributors an advantage, the tax system tends to put control of the churches into the hands of their richer, often more conservative members.

Then, there's the question of money given to the churches by non-religious foundations. When the Rockefeller Foundation underwrites the training of theological students, or the Ford Foundation gives two billion dollars to Catholic colleges for faculty salaries, these are also public subsidies, since the foundations' incomes are also tax-free. According to one set of figures, about half the tax-free foundations' income goes to religious groups, which comes to several billion dollars a year. This heady sum may be exaggerated but there is no doubt that large quantities of money do arrive at churchly portals via the foundations and are, in part, courtesy of the ordinary citizen.

A smaller but still significant sort of assist to religion comes in the form of tax-exemptions for religious personnel. Protestant ministers and rabbis can deduct their rental allowances, including utilities and repairs. Priests, either by law or practice, are exempt from the income tax—religious-order priests because they have taken a vow of poverty and have no property, secular or diocesan priests because the bishop owns the church property in his name and the various fees collected by the priest go technically to him. Secular priests are, though, supposed to pay taxes on their non-church private incomes, but it's doubted whether, in practice, such funds are separated from the tax-free ones belonging to the church.

One survey puts the grand total of church holdings at $100 billion, counting real property, but no one knows for sure because churches are not obligated to tell even their own flocks. Their shyness in this respect is a quite striking contrast to their eager publicity on membership. A priest says, "The Church must be the biggest corporation in the United States . . . our assets and real estate holdings must exceed those of Standard Oil, ATT, and U.S. Steel combined," but there is no serious accounting. In snippets, from press cuttings and the like, one learns that the Knights of Columbus own Yankee Stadium; the Temple Baptist Church in Los Angeles owns the Auditorium Company, valued at several million dollars; the Catholic Church owns Potomac Plaza, a large residential development in Washington, D.C.; the Self-Realization Fellowship, a West Coast religious sect, a chain of restaurants known as the Mushroomburger; that denominations and churches own bookstores, textile mills, distilleries, even the mortgage on the home of Billie Sol Estes.

"In view of this favored tax position, with reasonably prudent management," says no less an authority than Eugene Carson Blake, former Stated Clerk, or chief executive, of the Presbyterian Church in the U.S.A. and now executive secretary of the World Council of Churches, "the churches ought to be able to control the whole economy of the nation in the predictable future."

The same organizations which can qualify for exemption from local property taxes are generally also exempt from federal taxes on income from interest, dividends, royalties, rent or capital gains, otherwise known as "unrelated business income." The system has meant, in practice, that the churches have an unparalleled opportunity for material enrichment in the business world. "If a church operates a business it pays no income tax, and most states follow the federal government on this," says Charles Whelan, S.J., of Fordham Law School, a leading authority on the subject. "Dioceses and fraternal lodges own property under the set-up. Technically, the churches must be in control of the business, but there are gimmicks." He adds dubiously, "Business is not the proper business of the churches."

"Lease backs" are one arrangement which shows how churches can get a large return on investments without risk. They can bid high for property because of their favorable tax position, and the business firm can continue to operate with capital free for something else. Such an instance involved three Bloomington, Illinois, churches—First Baptist, First Christian, Second Presbyterian— which marched into business without the expenditure of a single dollar. The churches bought, in 1952, for $3.5 million on paper, the Hotel Dayton Biltmore from Hilton Hotels Corporation. Wealthy pillars of the three churches pledged $200,000 in personal loans for the down payment, and the hotel was subsequently leased back to the Hilton chain with the rent applied against interest costs and the balance of the debt. The hotel was later transferred once again to the Hilton group, with a tax-free profit to the churches of $450,000. Everybody was happy, the churches, the businessmen, and perhaps God.

"Feeder corporations" can be set up by churches under assumed names to construct apartments, shopping centers, office buildings and so on. Under certain conditions not only the parent religious body but the feeder corporation itself is exempt from paying taxes or even filing a return.

Special low postage rates for religious publications, the salaries of chaplains in the armed forces, in prisons and in the U.S. House of Representatives or the Senate—there are myriad ways in which the state gives assistance to the churches. Some of these are traditional by now, and some do not involve money. For the state makes genuflections toward the altar when it gives draft exemptions to theological students and ministers, or when school board membership is religiously determined. In the City of New York, for instance, the nine-man school board is evenly divided between Catholics, Protestants and Jews. As usual, the odd-man-out is the secular citizen.

Down in its bones the state still seems to feel that "religious" people are somehow more—one gropes for the words—"trustworthy," "honest," "reliable"—*"religious!"* Such logic, at any rate, must have figured in the conventional wisdom of the Iowa court which, not long ago, compelled a child of a dead mother to live with its grandparents instead of a father, because he was "agnostic." In many states the laws specify—and religiously identified judges go even further in insisting—that a child be adopted not only by religious parents but by those of the same faith. Partly, the practice is justified "for the child's own good"—his entree to the kingdom of heaven—and when the parents are dead, by saying that this is the choice they would have made. But there is no doubt that religion's search for members is thereby rewarded, and, says Leo Pfeffer, a foremost U.S. authority on church-state relations, "judicial protection is sought not for the parent but for the religion. . . . It is a questionable assumption that a deceased parent would have chosen religious continuity rather than temporal happiness and welfare for the child."

Indeed, adoption procedures are a striking example of the conflict of secular and religious values. For because of the restrictions the matching of parents and children is sometimes difficult, and the child, waiting for the right fit, may pass out of early infancy and not be adopted at all. Many adoption agencies, chafing at this result, enter into a gentle conspiracy with adoptive parents and understanding ministers. The parents "join" a church, the minister writes a letter saying so, the agencies pass the letter to the judge and the child is adopted, though the parents have never and will never set foot in church.

Religious ideas, of course, are apparent in laws affecting divorce, birth control, and abortions, and attempts to change them continue to meet fierce, often crippling churchly resistance, usually Catholic-led.[2] (That a well-organized minority can control a loose secular majority is clearly shown in the state of Israel, where, though it's estimated that no more and probably less than 10 per cent of the population is deeply religious, the religious laws continue to obtain, though many people, probably a vast majority, regard them as highly irksome, *e.g.*, there are no busses on Saturdays in some Israeli cities.) Courts and legislatures, bowing to religious pressures, confer on the churches the mantle of custodian of the nation's morality. The practical result of the regulations is often to force people into complicated law-evasion techniques, and the principal victims of rectitude are the same people the churches say they want most to help, the poor, who don't know how, or can't afford, to get around the laws.

Church control over laws governing morality, it can be antici-

---

[2] Just how fierce the pressures can be is indicated in the case of Mrs. Madelyn Murray, now Mrs. O'Hair, who instituted the successful antischool-prayer suit in Maryland in 1960. Mrs. Murray, immediately on filing suit, lost a seventeen-year job with the Baltimore welfare department. She says that she and her whole family were the subjects of abuse, vandalism of her home, obscene telephone calls, beatings of her two sons at school. Even after the Supreme Court decided in her favor in 1963, the pressure continued, perhaps because she was beginning another suit, to force religious bodies to pay taxes on their holdings, and then, she is a self-proclaimed atheist. Accused of encouraging a girl to renounce her religion for atheism (the girl later married her son), and after what Mrs. Murray has said was a violent struggle with the police, who knocked down her seventy-three-year-old mother with a billy club, Mrs. Murray was arrested, released on bail and fled Maryland, after which she faced still more legal harassment.

pated with confidence, will gradually diminish to the vanishing point as the claims of secular man are recognized and as religious organizations abandon their distinctive positions. "One of our major aims is to change the laws on abortions, divorce and so on," says an Episcopal reformer in New York. "After all, the churches are responsible for getting them passed." The churches, especially the liberal churches, have already begun to switch their bets from moral formation to welfare and human rights. And here they have gained a new and powerful ally—a *deus ex machina* appearing on the scene just when organized religion needed it most—the federal government.

The new chapter in church-state relations began after World War II when the government started using churches as administrators and beneficiaries of massive federal funds. Today, says Dr. George LaNoue, "Separation of church and state is not an accurate descriptive phrase. Under current federal programs, a church institution can obtain its land from the Department of the Interior; its buildings and equipment from the Department of Health, Education and Welfare via the General Services Administration; its mortgage insurance from the Housing and Home Finance Agency; its food from the Department of Agriculture; and its liquor from the Treasury. Should it encounter an act of God, the church institution can turn to the Small Business Administration for a disaster loan. This is something less than an absolute wall of separation between church and state."[3]

Participating to this extent in the "federal policy process" has led the churches into some startling and perhaps insoluble contradictions. For instance, under the Hospital Survey and Construction Act of 1946, otherwise known as the Hill-Burton Act, church hospitals have large federal assistance for equipment. Catholic hospitals alone got more than $200 million through 1960. Even hospitals run by Baptists—the staunchest advocates of a complete

---

[3] George R. LaNoue, *The Politics of Church and State* (New Haven: Yale University Press, 1968). LaNoue's new book is a very important contribution, and I am much indebted to the author for much of the material in the next few pages, which he showed me in manuscript.

church-state separation among the religious groups—have in some cases accepted Hill-Burton funds. Hospitals may accept such funds because they could not survive as constituted without them. And yet, federally underwritten though they are, the hospitals try to maintain their *religious* identity. Jewish hospitals continue to serve kosher food unless the patient specifically requests otherwise. Seventh Day Adventist hospitals, federally supported, ban smoking and serve a vegetarian diet—a steak must be prescribed by a doctor. Catholic hospitals may pipe services into the rooms, preserve Catholic laws on therapeutic abortion and sterilization, or insist that administrators and doctors be of the faith. "By what right," asked a lonely voice in a confidential memorandum circulated to policy-makers at the NCC, "may a church or church agency deny to any citizen the services his taxes pay for, or employment provided in the same way? Can a church hospital refuse to employ nurses, attendants, or physicians of other faiths than its own, when the funds out of which it pays employees and built its buildings came largely out of taxes paid under compulsion of law by all the citizens?"

There was a reason once for sectarian hospitals, when, say, Jewish doctors could not intern in Christian ones, or Jewish patients get in. Today, though, Jewish doctors can intern anywhere —or almost—and the Jewish hospitals' beds are largely occupied by non-Jewish patients. The name outside still reads Beth Israel or St. Mary's, from which the religious organizations get a reputation for mercy and charity, but they do remarkably little to merit the praise. Church organizations generally contribute only 3 to 5 per cent of the budgets of their own hospitals (and colleges). By far the largest part of their income is from fees charged for services with the government, in one form or another, making up the deficit. With programs like Medicare, the government share can be expected to grow.

What's true of hospitals is also the case with religiously run old-age homes. Largely on federal money, for instance, the Protestants more than doubled their "Golden Age" institutions between

1961 and 1967, and most such institutions get injections of government money, including local help. In these homes, Jews are said to feel more comfortable with Jews, Protestants with Protestants, Catholics with Catholics, and generally, only people of the same faith (to say nothing of color) are accepted. This was the principal reason why, under religious group pressure, the word "religion" was quietly omitted from the Civil Rights Act of 1965, so that under programs receiving federal funds discrimination was barred only on the grounds of race, color or nation origin. Without discrimination, clearly, the homes could not survive as *Jewish*, *Catholic* or *Protestant* homes, but without government funds they could not survive, either.

Sensibility for the feelings of organized religion seems to have dictated that "private" or "non-public" be used in government policy descriptions, but nonetheless, as of 1965, there were 115 federal programs in which churches could participate. The Treasury gives confiscated wines and liquors to churches; the Office of Economic Opportunity's Project Headstart uses church buildings and pays for upkeep; under the recreation or urban renewal programs the churches can buy land with cheap loans; the National Institutes of Health awarded a large grant to Western Reserve University in Cleveland for internships for clergymen in urban ministries; even the Department of Agriculture was conducting a seminar called "The Christian Farmer and His Country" while rural churches were asked to observe "Soil Stewardship Week." "It is doubtful," writes Dr. LaNoue, "that there is a legislature in the land so tongue-tied that it could not find a multitude of secular purposes to cover any religious interest it wished to accommodate."

Virtually nothing has been said in print about a government program which has benefitted the churches substantially—the disposal of real and surplus property, of which $4.5 billion's worth has been disposed of since 1944. Surplus property was supposed to be given to civic as well as religious groups—to cities, for instance, for education or recreation—but, says the National

Council of Churches, religious organizations got the lion's share of it (just as federal money has favored church-related hospitals over public ones). The Catholic Church has gotten more than half of all surplus property disposed of (even monasteries have received it), and it may be an indication of how much property the government is parcelling out that in Pennsylvania, in the year 1963 alone, the Catholic Church was the beneficiary of a million dollar's worth. When such properties had to be paid for, the rates charged public agencies were half again as much as what church organizations paid, and the churches were given low-cost loans, even as cities fought bitterly for space to relieve the pressure on their troubled ghettoes.

The friendliness of church and state domestically has been matched by their cooperation on international matters. Religious groups, for instance, can be formed in an area one might least expect them—immigration. The churches have fought for broader, more humanitarian immigration laws, but given a hand in the selection, they have displayed a more orthodox vision. What, one wonders, would the national composition of the U.S. have been today if in the eighteenth and nineteenth centuries the churches had had the power they were given under the Displaced Persons Act or the U.S. Escapee Program of 1952? For those who came, assurances of jobs and housing were required, and 90 per cent of the Displaced Persons were guaranteed them by voluntary agencies, primarily the churches. The U.S. Escapee Program was designed to lure defectors from behind the Iron Curtain and as such it was, clearly, an instrument of American foreign policy at the time. With a few exceptions the churches felt no qualms about participating: "Our attitude," says a churchman who was involved in the program, "was that our actions were justified on the grounds of the greater good of humanity." It was no accident that most of the refugees who arrived here identified themselves as "religious." Take the famous Hungarian refugees. Almost entirely handled by voluntary agencies, the Hungarians who were in trouble with church communities at home, who didn't profess a religious faith or who had been divorced arrived on these shores in far fewer numbers than those who met the standards of churchly perfection.

To the clasped-hands-across-the-sea on the Agency for International Development's food parcels might be added a third hand for the churches; indeed, the relationship is made explicit by the names of the Church World Service or the Catholic Relief Service, which appear on the boxes below AID's emblem. Under AID's Food for Peace program, the government provides the food and the ocean transportation while CWS (Protestant), CRS and CARE (non-sectarian) furnish internal transportation and personnel, although sometimes the government may even pay for these, and some churches want it to pay for the entire program. As it is, the federal government's share of the Catholic commodity program is 77 per cent, which means that government provides more than $100 million a year in food for the Catholic agency to distribute. For the Protestants the figure is about $10,500,000, and this, plus a reimbursement for ocean freight, plus another $500,000 for resettling Cuban refugees, comes to about 40 per cent of the Church World Service's budget. CWS, it's true, raises about $15 million in donated food, clothing, and so on, but the actual cash contribution of Protestant religion is less than a fifth of the federal one.

The voluntary agencies make estimates of how American food should be allocated, and while these are reviewed by government officials they are rarely changed. The result is that American food gifts sometimes follow the cross, if churches have historic ties with certain countries. Italy, with a population of under 50 million, received $50 million dollars of American surplus under Food for Peace between 1954 and 1960, 84 per cent of it through Catholic relief. In the same period, with ten times the population, India got less.

The churches aren't supposed to proselytize with government food but the name of a religious organization on a food package might be considered seductive and evidently the temptation to gain converts has not always been resisted. In Vietnam, AID briefly cut off supplies to the Catholic Relief Service, insisting on reforms. The abuse wasn't stated but it was said to be food favoritism to Catholics or those who would promise to join the faith.[4] The Catholics, in any case, are less doctrinaire about church-state separation than the Protestants, and more recently, were willing to supply, in lieu of wages that hadn't been paid by the government of South Vietnam, American food to several hundred thousand South Vietnamese pacification workers.

To some constitutional authorities these new ties have all but demolished a major American tradition, the wall of separation between church and state, and yet the destruction has been going on quietly, unimpeded by public protest or resistance from the churches themselves, who, it seems, look the other way. A survey of voluntary agencies, mainly religious, showed that some 41 per cent accepted tax funds, 5 per cent refused, and 53 per cent had no policy. But 61 per cent of those with "no policy" in fact accepted government money, which would seem to mean both a policy and an uneasiness about admitting it.[5] There can be little doubt why, when some "voluntary" church-related agencies receive 70, 80 or even 100 per cent of their total budgets from public tax money. "Not only are many sectarian agencies accepting tax funds through contractual agreements not based on a thought-out policy," says Father Bernard J. Coughlin, "but frequently also their practices are in spite of the policy indecision of higher executives, and sometimes even contrary to their policy decisions."[6]

It's true, of course, that some churches think the government has a duty to help them out, regarding the "wall" as less than sacred. "The separation of church and state," says a knowledgeable priest, "is but a negative moment in the dialectic of history,

[4] LaNoue, op. cit., p. 70.
[5] Bernard J. Coughlin, Church and State in Social Welfare (New York: Columbia University Press, 1965).
[6] Ibid., p. 74.

though it may take a thousand years to work out." The Catholic approach to church-state relations is embodied in the principle of "subsidiarity," the idea that it's a disturbance of what Catholics call "right order" to let a body of greater social rank perform services which could be delegated to "lesser bodies on a lower plane," as one Pope put it. The Catholics think that the churches should be given money and authority by the state because they perform a service of value. Just what the churches have to offer is described by a 1963 Lutheran report to the National Council of Churches. The churches help the state by offering prayer on its behalf, contributing to civil consensus in support of the state, encouraging responsible citizenship and government service, "holding [the state] accountable to the sovereign law of God," and championing human and civil rights. In return for such favors, the state aids the churches by acknowledging the sovereignty of God, being neutral toward church bodies, providing "incidental" benefits on the basis of the churches' services to the state and financial aid on a "non-preferential basis to church agencies engaged in social services which are of secular benefit to the community."

The pressure upon the churches to accept such arguments and to bite the apple of federal money is intense, even for those churchly bodies which view the state with distrust. Take those arch-separationists, the Southern Baptists. "Denominational heresy!" they cried when a Florida Baptist hospital accepted federal funds, and yet the problem is how to get along without. "The Baptists have a dilemma," says J. L. Sullivan, an authoritative Southern Baptist spokesman. "If we don't accept federal funds our colleges and hospitals will have trouble surviving. If we do, they have the difficulty of remaining distinctive and even justifying their very existence. But either we go the route of taking federal money or we shall have to close some doors."

There is, then, the challenge of simply maintaining the institutions which already exist, the old-age homes, the hospitals, the day schools, all of which need outside help because the denominations can no longer support them. If the Roman Catholic Church, though rich, can honestly cry poor, it's because their parochial school system, its facilities often out-of-date, requires heavy cash injections. And the precedents for taking public money are already established. "How," Dean M. Kelley, Director of the NCC's Commission on Religious Liberty, once asked the Protestants, "can you oppose aid to the Catholic parochial schools when your colleges and hospitals have been taking federal money for years?"

What also makes even the virgin denominations susceptible to the federal lure is organized religion's very weakness in the United States. Shrinking numbers of adherents, the conservatism and financial retentiveness of the parishioners, the need of the churches to show their muscle in an increasingly alien and secular world—all these have led to a kind of churchly low self-esteem. As Dr. LaNoue puts it, ". . . the churches' traditional theological and sacramental roles have been undermined to the extent that clergymen find reassurance in the government's invitation to join in welfare programs." To be relevant in the way the churches conceive it takes federal funds. And the government, after all, has beckoned the churches into the temple.

The pattern which has emerged is neither the establishment of religion or the separation of church and state, but a pragmatic arrangement with something for everybody. The government strengthens the churches and helps them continue their old charitable traditions, while the churches are supposed to generate support for government programs. Conservative legislators like the churches, and the liberals see them as buffers against the conservatives. For politicians of both camps, church support may mean votes.

But this is not the whole story, not quite. For just as the Catholic principle of subsidiarity assumes that everybody belongs to a religious group, so the new formula for church-state relations neglects the secular citizen. Take the archetypical case, the parochial schools. The Catholics want their schools subsidized, partly or altogether, on the grounds that it's unfair to ask them to pay for education which otherwise the state would have to provide. But maintaining a dual system of education would obviously be far more expensive, it would divert money from other public institutions, and it would set up a competing system of education which might be removed from public scrutiny, policy, or standards. For this the church would ask the secular citizen to foot the bill.

Further, the arrangement really means that the government is increasingly in the position of legitimizing and strengthening religion, and many churchmen shudder at the thought that once the federal camel gets his nose under the church tent he will want the rest of him inside, too. "When an institution depends upon certain sources of support more than others," says Dean Kelley, "it becomes metabolically related to them, almost continuous with them, in the way a tree is with its sources of water. . . . The churches should consider, before linking themselves with an almost irreversible pattern of symbiosis, whether their greatest contribution to meeting human need, shaping society, combating poverty and other ills, and transforming culture, is not predicated on their being genuinely different, distinctive, and free from other institutions." He goes on: "The churches may insist that no strings are attached to taking government money, but once they get it they want it again. This means that they won't do anything to offend prospective contributors."

The end results that some anxious churchmen foresee are tame churches, their prophetic voices either stilled or stripped of credibility, their modern edifices paid for by public money, their organizations shaped by tax dollars (the Church World Service, for instance, has grown with its federal funds from a small office in the National Council of Churches to the major item in the budget), their role, as an NCCer puts it, "nothing but managers of a quasi-religious enterprise. Our problem now is to keep the government from buying the churches outright."

It's sometimes asked whether involvement in government programs has not given the churches a vested interest in the poor, and indeed, the subtle shift away from the word "charity" to "philanthropy" and finally "non-profit," to "client" for the recipient of such favors, reveals a distinct nervousness on religion's part. For charity, some say, is degrading—to the giver and the receiver both. "Charity has a long and noble history, but the time has long come to begin to say farewell to alms and to replace it with the rights of citizenship," writes Dr. Pfeffer. He goes on: "The churches should get out of welfare, lock, stock and barrel, not just because of the unconstitutionality of many present church-state relations but because welfare, inevitably, is charity and we must now substitute rights for charity."

Some authorities argue that secularized charities whose purposes are non-sectarian, like many Jewish agencies, provide a proper compromise between church-state separation on the one hand and human need on the other. But, they say, the secular agency must be careful not to attempt to further religious or religious-cultural aims.

One proposal has it that the government should not use churches when secular agencies can do the job, and another is to turn all church-related agencies, including colleges, into secular ones, with no connection with organized religion at all. Such steps, say the prophets, would cut through the terrible contradictions in modern church-state relations, alleviate the charge that the secular citizen's unwanted charity is, in fact, organized religion, and make the churches independent, once and for all. But it would also mean that church organizations would shrink to their true size and influence, a radical transformation in religion's ideas about marching into the world. Considering how strongly the churches want to get there, it does not seem likely that this prophetic message will be heard.

Chapter Eight

God-a-Go-Go

ST. MARK'S IN-THE-BOWERY

*Friday (tomorrow), a multi-media Christmas pro-
gram, "Quasar," will be given at 9:15 p.m. in the
church. The program will include psychedelic slides
and films, dance, and a musical collaboration of Indian
sitar, organ, flute and brass. The program, dedicated to
the peoples of Vietnam, will be repeated Thursday,
Dec. 29 and Friday, Dec. 30.*
          —THE (GREENWICH) VILLAGE VOICE

WHAT in heaven have quasars to do with psychedelic slides, Indian sitars with the peoples of Vietnam, or any of the above with a
church service? The clue, of course, is to be found in the word
"relevance," for some in the churches literally the last hope on
earth.

Within living ecclesiastical memory there has always been tension between those like Billy Graham who believe in gradual
efforts to change the world, and those who would boldly seize the
secular bull by the horns, even if traditional church doctrines and
attitudes had to be changed, too. In 1914, Walter Rauschenbush,

a famous Baptist preacher, was urging religion to accept "the new social enthusiasm," and a generation later, Reinhold Niebuhr told Christians to abandon perfectionism, accept guilt and dirty their hands in public affairs. Having been heard momentarily, the churches fell silent again after World War II, as they became more democratically responsive to their essentially conservative parishioners. In ecclesiastical annals, the 1950's may well go down as the age of churchly conformity, when American religion was famous worldwide for its unslakable thirst for new members and insatiable appetite for new churches.

As for social issues, a sort of Missouri Compromise was worked out. As expressed by one of its partisans, Prof. W. Widick Schroeder of the Chicago Theological Seminary, "The prophetic side of religion can and should be institutionalized in the hierarchy without disturbing the local Church. On the parish level religion should be adjustive and integrative, supporting monogamy, democracy and modified free enterprise. I see the proper role of the pastor as one of passionate moderation."

Beyond real doubt the mass of American churchgoers would agree with this formulation, but for a sizable few it contains a contradiction, if not schizophrenia. For, they say, the churches are asked to be two-faced, with the constituents mouthing one brand of religion and the leadership articulating quite another. Not only were the dissidents unhappy but there were also pressing institutional reasons for squaring the contradiction. Public apathy was one, for conventional, church-on-Sunday religion simply wasn't pulling them in. And among ministers and churchly bureaucrats—extending, perhaps, to the very top—there was a perceptible disenchantment with the uses of American religion in the world of the 1960's. "Many people here feel trapped," says Rufus Cornelson, Associate General Secretary of the National Council of Churches. "They may rationalize by saying that it's always like that in a bureaucracy, but the problem is somewhat unique for churchmen and it goes deeper than we are willing to admit. There is disillusionment, a sense of despair, with regard to the effectiveness of our leadership and mission. Our optimism, I fear, is often fabricated."

There has come to pass a veritable outpouring of literature designed to lead the churches out of the wilderness and set them on the straight path—to name a few: *They Call Us Dead Men, The Noise of Solemn Assemblies, Honest to God, The Comfortable Pew, The Suburban Captivity of the Churches, A Modern Priest Looks at His Outdated Church.* One of the key words of this kind is *The Secular City*, by a young Baptist theologian and Harvard professor of religion named Harvey Cox. Though Cox's ideas were by no means new to church intellectuals, they seemed to catch the essence of what the critics were saying and to speak to religionists of every creed.

For Cox the collapse of traditional religion, far from being a controversial matter, is a characteristic feature of the time. What we have, instead, is the age of secularization, the liberation of man from religious and metaphysical tutelage, an epoch of no religion at all. "The gods of traditional religions live on as private fetishes of the patrons of congenial groups," he says, "but they play no role whatever in the public life of the secular metropolis."

But Cox is writing to a religious, not a secular audience, and thus feels compelled to prove that secularization has biblical justification and authority. The secular or urban style of life is evidently one the religious population still has some difficulty accepting, for Cox is at pains to prove that anonymity—what E. B. White once called "the gift of privacy"—is not necessarily bad. People in big cities are not really unfriendly, although they may be busy and selective, and though they may reject Christian fellowship, the pamphlets and the comforting Word. Characteristically, too, they are mobile, but being "on the go," as Cox calls it, is an American attribute, and indeed, has been preached by great American writers like Melville, Mark Twain and *Joseph Conrad*. (One trusts that Cox is a better theological than literary scholar.) In short, the pragmatic, secular way—exemplified by John F. Kennedy and Albert Camus, who are the "personifications of the

buoyant reasonableness and calm sense of assurance which characterized the best in our epoch"—is not only the dominant but an
attractive, worthy style of life.

As gently as possible, providing familiar cushions to ease the
shocks, Cox wants to usher religious men into the apse of secular
society. For when he gets there, religious man, like the sleeper of
H. G. Wells who arises in a nightmare of the future, discovers a
strange world of people who don't require ontological explanations of existence, who don't ask ultimate questions, who don't, as
religious people do, experience "the shock and terror of those who
wake in the night to find their whole theistic faith has been built
on a conjecture" because the secular man never had a theistic
faith to start with. The era of the sacred society is over. The
Christian should abandon any thought of trying to resacralize it—
quite the reverse, his job is to see that the society stays secular and
does not convert its secular ideology into a new religion, intolerant
of traditional ones. Christians, then, like Jews, have become the
minority and require the tolerance of the outside world.

Having established the authority of secular values for religious
man, who has always been accustomed to being in the majority,
Cox turns to the central question confronting the churches—what
are they to do in this new world, what justifications can they give
for continuing to exist? The answers cannot be found by the author in traditional religious interpretations. "Our doctrines of the
church," he says, "have come to us from the frayed-out period
of classical Christendom and are infected with the ideology of
preservation and permanence. They are almost entirely past-
oriented, deriving their authority from one or another classical
period, from an alleged resemblance to some earlier form of
church life, or from a theory of historical continuity. But this will
no longer do."

The churches, instead, must elect social change and a theology
to go with it. Cox means, specifically, "revolutionary social
change," which he says is not merely a willingness to act but to be
born again (perhaps in the manner of Luther's resolution of his
identity crisis through his "rebirth" as a theologian), to see things

in a wholly new perspective. Old attitudes must be discarded and new ones invented as man sheds his adolescence. He must follow the Gospel summons to "frame with his neighbor a common life suitable to the secular city." The churches are to be "God's avant-garde." Cox says elsewhere that "the Christian transforms culture by plunging fearlessly into its thought processes" and, fearlessly plunging, he discusses the role of this avant-garde in terms like "getting where the action is" and "locating today's action." The churches must ally themselves with the world on the fronts of civil rights, poverty, and the meaning of work, leisure and sex. (He seems more preacherly than revolutionary when he says, ". . . we must avoid giving a simple yes-or-no answer to the question of premarital chastity. Of course, this will sound like evasion. . . .")

It may be a measure of the distance separating the new social religionists like Cox and the traditional parishes, that nowhere in *The Secular City* is there mention of church services, prayer or other customary religious observances. There should even be, Cox says, a moratorium in talking about God. Indeed, for a critic like Rabbi Richard L. Rubenstein, Coxian theology lacks serious roots. "The prophetic role of religion as a social catalyst is quite secondary," Rubenstein says in *The Secular City Debate*. "Religion cannot be indifferent to social justice but neither can its major task be equated with its pursuit. The primary role of religion is priestly." But, for Cox, reflecting a feeling common to Protestant ministers, the priestly role has lost allure. ("Suppose you're a minister," an NCC official said to me. "You've got a small amount of faith and a vague commitment to doing good. So you preach social justice.")

"What else *can* the churches do than recognize and proclaim what God is doing in the world?" asks a special commission of the World Council of Churches (italics mine). Religion, it says, should give up all idea of self-aggrandizement, forgetting about statistics; it must cease to proselytize; it should adopt the messianic life in the form of a servant church, ministering to others. The "waiting-church" should be replaced by "go-structures."

The go-go urge of modern religion has taken a wide variety of forms, from the extreme to the relatively mild, from the Death of God to coffee houses and the twist in the aisles. Sitars and quasars, eclectic, perhaps bizarre assortments of the far out and the way in—some churchmen seem almost desperate to be contemporary. Take the little prayer from *Are You Running with Me, Jesus?* by Malcolm Boyd:

> It's morning, Jesus. It's morning, and here's that light and sound all over again.
>
> I've got to move fast . . . get into the bathroom, wash up, grab a bite to eat, and run some more.
>
> I just don't feel like it, Lord. All I seem to want today is the big sleep, and here I've got to run all over again.
>
> Where am I running? You know these things I can't understand. It's not that I need to have you tell me. What counts most is just that somebody knows, and it's you. That helps a lot.
>
> So I'll follow along, OK? But lead, Lord. Now I've got to run. Are you running with me, Jesus?

One of the most original churches in America, hardly typical of either the American Baptists or United Church of Christ, with both of which it's affiliated, is Judson Memorial in New York City. After World War II the church found itself in the condition of a semi-retired man with plenty of means. It had a large endowment and a spacious building in Greenwich Village, but only a score of faithful members. It opened its doors to the neighborhood with a narcotics program and a guidance center, and then, as city services took over such programs, Judson became a home for the experimental arts, with a picture gallery and two theaters, one located in its sanctuary, where the only visible sign of religion today is a cross which is lowered from the ceiling on Sunday when its ministers conduct services in business suits. Some of the plays put on where Judson's altar once was could have caused an antipornographic panic at a typical church supper. "We could try theater, too," a pastor's wife said sarcastically to Al Carmines, one of Judson's ministers, who in the course of things has developed into a well-known local composer, "if *we* didn't mind beer cans on the church floor."

Howard Moody, the pastor of Judson, is one of a group of New York ministers who have been active in counseling unmarried pregnant girls and helping them find abortionists. The danger of prosecution is real, but Moody and the others have gone ahead. "The churches must do what's right, not what's respectable," Moody says. "I realize that by being so heavily involved in secular causes the church faces a definite risk in the loss of its separate identity. It's a risk I'm prepared to take, instead of hiding our insecurity in paternalism, arrogance and superstition."

In New York as in other metropolitan centers, many churches manage to stay in existence only through a combination of a few wealthy members, large endowments and tax exemptions. They go on, year after year, with traditional religion and empty pews. The reason they don't change is illustrated by the events at an Episcopal church in the heart of the Haight-Ashbury section of San Francisco. The rector converted a room used only for Sunday School into a twenty-four-hour-a-day counseling, medical and legal aid center staffed by volunteers. But the clients were hippies —some on LSD—and in protest the big contributors withheld their pledges and lay officials resigned.

There are probably no more than a dozen experimental churches like Judson throughout the U.S. Partly, at least, because the parishes insist on retaining their old identities, the thrust of in-the-worldliness for organized religion has come from the denominations, which have sometimes been forced to disguise their activities from the membership in complicated budget descriptions. Even so, the denominational contributions, either directly or through umbrella organizations like the NCC, have been exceedingly small in terms of total church budgets, although recently a few denominations have begun more elaborate programs directed to helping people in the slums, and there is heady talk among churchmen about "tactics" and "strategies" for changing the world. For some churchly dissidents, the only way for religion to aim itself toward secular society is to divest itself of all forms of traditional charities and activities—schools, hospitals, old-age homes and so forth—which, in any case, are largely financed by the government, but even if the leaders wanted to take this step, it's doubtful the members would let them.

Although the churches spend most of their money on themselves, they do, nonetheless, spent it, and a few denominations have tried to put teeth in their dollars. Several Catholic dioceses have Project Equality which tries to see that Catholic purchases are not made from firms which practice racial discrimination. The United Church of Christ sold its stock holdings in several companies which discriminated against Negroes and the Methodists withdrew ten million dollars from banks which made large loans to the Union of South Africa, in protest against *apartheid*. But the churches have generally found that business, the old whipping-boy of liberals, is just as interested in racial progress as they are.

Because both churchly targets and goals have remained elusive, the ecclesiastical accent has been on the word "experimental." ("The denominations say 'experimental' so as not to be blamed if they fail," an inner-city minister claims tartly.) Broadly speaking, the denominational experiments have taken two forms: One of these is the so-called experimental or specialized minister who, loosely or non-affiliated with a particular church, tries to reach particular social groups. There are shopping-center ministers, ministers for homosexuals, for depressed women awaiting divorce in Las Vegas, skiers at Squaw Valley, California, and alcoholics. The churches were excited at the thought of a specialized ministry reaching up to the unchurched hordes living in high-rise apartment buildings. The attempts to woo the faithless failed, but the churchmen did discover an interesting phenomenon which theologians might well ponder: The higher you live in a building the less concerned you are with religion.

An example of a specialized pastor is a Lutheran named Ralph Gensel, who tries to minister to jazz musicians in New York City. For the last ten years, though a non-drinker, Gensel has spent three nights a week or so at night clubs, sometimes sitting at his table until closing time, making himself available for advice and counsel. Gensel wants to prove the churches are "with it," and he says proudly, "If I get on a TV show, that's ministry!"

Not so content—and just as typical—was the young Presbyterian in Macon, Georgia, who had been sent to help the Negro community. Discouraged, he blamed himself because he had been able to reach a few Negro children with reading lessons but no Negro adults. Most of the time he tried to help prostitutes and derelicts. Once a week the tiny group met at the alcoholic mission, a nice lady sat down at the piano, and they sang:

> Earthly friends may prove untrue,
> Doubts and fears assail;
> One still loves and cares for you:
> One who will not fail.
> Jesus never fails,
> Jesus never fails . . .

These ecclesiastical loners may be brave and self-sacrificing men, but they represent a miniscule outlay in religious cash and personnel.

Another way the churches have tried to be relevant is through ministerial teams, working on specialized projects. The largest is the Delta Ministry, with a more than $100,000 budget from the NCC and individual denominations, plus U.S. government help. Operating in one of the poorest sections of the country, the Mississippi delta, these missionaries for relevance distribute donated clothing and government surplus food and try to get Negroes to exercise their rights through the ballot. Since the 1920's the churches have also run ministries for migrant workers in thirty-eight states. The largest of these, the California Migrant Ministry, illustrates well the perils of relevance for organized religion. "The basic relationship between that part of the community we [Christians] represent and the labor camps and fringe areas is one of exploitation. We live well at the expense of these field workers and their families. They provide cheap labor. . . . Their low status feeds our sense of well-being. Our pride is their humiliation," Rev. Wayne C. Hartmire, Jr., the fiery director of the migrant ministry, told church people. When he began actively supporting striking grape workers, contributions from the local churches fell off sharply, and the cries went up that Hartmire should be preaching the Gospel, not social action. "I feel it's dishonest to do traditional welfare without attacking the causes. On balance," Hartmire says, "the churches are more a force for the perpetuation of the status quo than changing it, but the denominations—as opposed to parishes—do show some ability to transcend their self-interest, in limited ways, that most institutions in our society don't."

The prime target of relevance-minded religionists has been the so-called inner city. Action groups of all kinds have spawned, dedicated to helping the poor, especially the Negro poor, to fomenting interracial brotherhood, and to winning a place for Christian ideals in modern industrial society. One churchly response, in a dozen cities, was the formation of what are called industrial missions, such as the Chesapeake Foundation, which tries to carry on a Christian dialogue with public officials, the Detroit Industrial Mission which has been active in convincing the automobile companies to undertake the training of unskilled Negro workers, the Community Renewal Society (once the Chicago City Missionary Society) which has organized boycotts, started summer camps, conducted training in non-violence, investigated settlement houses and tried to usher poor people through the maze of bureaucracy so that they might obtain the rights and benefits available to them under the law. "Our object is not charity," says the mission's director, Don Benedict, "but to put money and responsibility into the hands of those who need it."

"The idea is to illuminate, provoke and summon secular institutions to their calling and vocation," says Jitsuo Morikawa, the director of Metropolitan Associates of Philadelphia, or MAP, a mission concerned with urban life. Such activists want to infiltrate, and sometimes confront squarely, industrial society so as to make it more responsively generous to human need. One of the singularities of this effort is that the industrial missioners have almost no way to evaluate the success, or lack of it, of their attempts to introduce change. The Detroit Industrial Mission was once turned down for a foundation grant on the grounds that it couldn't describe its objectives. Still, by such yardsticks as there are, the industrial missions do not seem to have obtained spectacular results. By one estimate most missions reach no more than five hundred people a year, and the total production of new Christian leaders by all the industrial missions is less than the membership of one good-sized suburban church. Scott Paradise, a minister who now heads the Boston Industrial Mission but who for years worked in the DIM, kept a diary of his experience as a missioner deep in the jungle of industry, as he tried to convey to factory workers, union officials and management, the relevance of the faith. The environment, he senses, is hostile to him. It is guilty of idolatry by putting business needs ahead of Christian values. He thinks that by "stimulating thinking, asking questions and engaging in discussions, we could change attitudes even without a thoroughgoing attack on the system itself." Toward the end of his thousand-page journal he remembers, plaintively, how factory workers asked him not to return to their lunch table because the topic of Christianity, by them, had been adequately covered in a few discussions. "I remembered being thrown out of the Ford Public Relations Department for proposing to discuss questions which probed the ethics of PR practices." He recalls being no longer welcome in the Ford Stamping Division after he suggested guaranteed income for all as "a possible social goal toward which Christians might work. I remembered also the recent report evaluating two of our management discussion groups. The report gave the impression that [the] amount of changes in attitudes resulting from our discussions are so small as to be perhaps insignificant."

If religion has a hard time making itself heard above the clang of the assembly line it has not found the ghettoes easy going either. Such is the excitement at the possibilities of action for the Christian community that the demand on the part of Protestant ministers for inner-city jobs greatly exceeds the supply, and the trends don't indicate that the Christians will find a bigger role to play. Several awesome difficulties confront the modern missioners who would help the Negro and Spanish-speaking poor. Government welfare, constantly expanding, nibbles away at church programs, whether they be remedial reading or halfway houses for addicts, until there is less and less for the ecclesiastical in-the-worlders to offer. Churchmen profess not to be worried—their job, they claim, was to point the way—but as the possibilities for practical service diminish, the inner-city missions are pushed more and more into vaguer concepts like community action, "dialogue," "humanization" and so on. Here, Christian ideology begins to confront that of the Negro.

White religion, it seems, has never quite been able to shake off the charge of George Bernard Shaw that it "functions as a sort of auxiliary police force, taking the insurrectionary edge off poverty." In trying to validate their faith through action in the Negro communities, the whites also lay themselves open to accusations of faith exploitation. According to James P. Breeden, Director of the Commission on Religion and Race of the Massachusetts Council of Churches, a Negro himself, "The Negro saves the church from irrelevancy, but therefore a new round of exploitation begins. If my involvement with Negroes is to prove the churches are worth saving, then I am necessarily in an exploitative relationship, because the source of my involvement is to demonstrate my own worth. It's the old paternalism. This is why the idea of Black Power disturbs white church people. If I say I can do without you, it requires you to relate on a different basis." He goes on, "The announcement that the churches will do this or that for the ghetto comes to the Negro parish without any prior consultation with its minister. There are few signs of change."

A bellwether for Christian inner-city missions is the experience of the oldest of the new-style experimental groups, the East Harlem Protestant Parish in New York. Starting from scratch in 1948, when not a single church of a major white denomination existed in the area, the parish survived crisis after crisis until it became a full-fledged organization offering a credit union, remedial reading, summer camps and the like to a constituency estimated at eight thousand people. In 1967, on the verge of its twentieth birthday, the parish ran into trouble. Its literature had once referred to East Harlem as a "Gift of the City. . . . In the very act of confronting us in the city with the failure of our old patterns, God is reminding us that we must look again, as did our Reformation ancestors, for His patterns for the new day in which we live." It was hard to believe the East Harlemite regarded himself as a "gift"; indeed, there was, to those who turned against the parish, something essentially white, self-justifying, paternalistic, and old-style missionary in such an approach. "The East Harlem Protestant *Plantation*," a white staff member said contemptuously. And the parish's leadership *was* almost exclusively white—even the parish workers were white. Negroes, it seemed, were unwilling to work for the low salaries offered, just as the self-sacrificing whites appeared to glory in them. Dialogue, reconciliation, brotherhood—"The white churches are hung up on a desire to be an integrated community just when the Negroes want to be themselves," says Rev. George Webber, a well-known inner-city theoretician and a founder of the parish. For the white leadership it was just as unChristian for blacks to emphasize their separateness and exclusiveness as it was for whites to do so down South, yet for many in the East Harlem black community the ministry was carrying out a "negative witness" by preempting Negro leadership. Only by occupying the top positions themselves, by gaining experience with power and pressing for their own solutions, could the Negroes rise, they said. Torn by controversy, confronting diminished contributions from white churches fearful of black power and increasing disinterest by the larger black community, the survival of this pioneering Christian effort was clearly uncertain.

In New York, Rev. Webber heads a group called MUST, standing for Metropolitan Urban Service Training, which puts ministers and laymen through a stiff course on city problems. Webber is frank to admit that MUST "is concerned with the terrific defection rate from the Protestant ministry" and, he thinks, experimental programs like his own may be virtually the last hope for many a waverer within church ranks. But he goes on, "My own idea is that if the churches could rid themselves of overt or covert paternalism, if they could only drop all ulterior motives for power, organizational success, converts and so on, then they could be free, and Christian witness, mission, whatever you want to call it, would define itself. My feeling is that the ministerial dropouts, working in ordinary jobs, are the clergy of the future."

For all their tribulations in the inner city, the Protestants have nonetheless taken the white religious leadership there. "The Jews," says Irving M. Levine, Director of Education and Urban Planning for the American Jewish Committee, "aren't as relevant as they used to be. Rhetoric, ideology played a great role in the early days of civil rights and the Jews were good at such things. In recent years we've proved far less effective as activists. We've had a style of involvement and it's hard to retool. It's the white Protestant ministers in the slums who are the new heroes for many Jews. It's true, I think, that Jews have turned in upon themselves. One reason, certainly, is the feeling we're no longer needed, because the Negro leadership in many cases has turned against us, and indeed, tends to view us as an oppressor class. It's interesting to note that about the one thing Negroes turn to us for today is advice on fund-raising, at which we excel. Another reason for the Jewish retreat is that so many Jews live in suburbs—do you know that not a single Jew has graduated from a Cleveland public high school in five years? Our lack of real involvement in the front lines is causing a terrible crisis in the Jewish leadership. This isn't to say that individual Jews aren't active, but they tend to be active outside the pale, not as representatives of Jewish religion and not even as members of the Jewish community."

Catholic participation on the front lines of the inner city has likewise been small. There are few Catholic experimental slum parishes and "probably no more than a hundred priests in the U.S. active full-time on experimental inner-city projects," according to

Philip Scharper, editor-in-chief of the Catholic publishing house Sheed and Ward. "The Protestants knew they had lost touch with the working classes and the poor, and the inner city was seen as a way of re-establishing contact. The Catholics thought they were already active in poverty areas through ethnic groups. We didn't realize that as Catholics moved from cities to suburbs a vacuum had been created—we, too, had lost touch with the inner city. There has been aroused a sudden sense of responsibility and a feeling of the need to justify Catholic existence through greater involvement in the trouble-spots."

Although the big denominations have recently stepped up their contributions to the inner city, it does not seem that their involvement in the urban arena has been a spectacular success, at least in its new forms, for all the bravery displayed by a few ministerial firebrands. If the churches can't be blamed for failing to solve the enormous urban mess in the United States, it's still true that religion saw, in the cities, a unique opportunity to test out its new ideas of being in the world. The failure of these ideas to take hold—either in the world or among the bulk of church members —has led to a perceptible drift on the part of the dissidents toward getting out of the denominations altogether, to working in the government anti-poverty programs or to joining one of the new experimental communities. Existing generally outside the denominations, scorning American churches for triviality, these groups may have an importance which transcends their numbers, for they point a direction which American religion could conceivably follow.

These new bands, of which there are no more than a few dozen in the U.S., have certain characteristics in common: They are Protestant; they despair of organized denominational religion; they are unconventional, at least by traditional standards; they believe in discipline; unlike the withdrawing, privatised groups like the Amish, they live mostly in cities and they want, above all, to make an impact on contemporary life, partly by actions and partly by example. One such community is the Church of the Savior in

Washington, D. C. Its members really are card-carrying Christians, since they do carry signed cards pledging them to the rules of the church—regular prayer (pick your own), steady attendance, personal integrity. You must give, once you have passed a stringent examination and been accepted for membership, 10 per cent of your income before taxes, and this is why the church, with a membership of only eighty, can support five full-time staff people, run a coffee house and a farm, and conduct a program for teaching underprivileged children in the slums. The character of the church—intense, conservative devotionally, but liberal in social view, demanding that the Christian life be *lived*—is a far cry from the ordinary parish and hardly a way many Americans would follow. Among the Savior's members is James Rouse, the community developer, and it's no accident that the church planned for Rouse's new city, Columbia, Maryland, will be non-denominational and operate out of a community center.

Ekklesia, in Rochester, New York, is a non-denominational community dedicated to better housing, while Secular Christian Ventures in Cayahoga Falls, Ohio, the result of the influence of a former pastor there, William Dudley (whose expulsion from a more conventional church was discussed in Chapter Three), concentrates its efforts in a counseling center in downtown Cleveland. The group which has reached the largest number of people is the Ecumenical Institute in Chicago, which in 1968 would run forty thousand Americans through its concentrated, forty-four-hour study program in theological education, aimed at renewing Christian thought. The focus of the effort is, of course, the inner city, and the Ecumenical Institute has undertaken a community reorganization project in a sixteen-block Chicago area. The Institute believes that what is wrong with American cities is the lack of community, and its ideal city, laid away as yet in heaven, would be built thus, brick by brick, out of small bands, highly organized and dedicated to a communal Christian life.

The engine of this effort is what the Institute calls its "Order," a group of a hundred and fifty interracial adults which comprises the faculty, all of whom live the communal life in urban Chicago, raising their children collectively, rising six days a week at 6:15 A.M. to worship, eating in a common mess, and pooling their financial resources. The Institute thinks that religion will follow its lead, moving away from ritualistic parishes into groups of believers whose concentration is not on themselves but on the broader community; indeed, they see no other hope.

Whether such thinking is forward to the future needs of people or backward to the small town is open to doubt, but some Christians are clearly willing to defy the concensus, to interpret the faith in novel ways. Said an ad in *The Christian Century*:

IF YOU HAVE READ
TALKED
PREACHED ABOUT LAY MINISTRY

HOW ABOUT PRACTICING IT?

Many clergymen today face the frustration of being unable to bring about the renewal of the Congregational-Denominational-Establishment (CDE), and yet feel TRAPPED because they believe they are neither qualified for secular jobs, nor are they sure what alternative there is to the CDE. Come and be a part of the chaos—with us.

The Sycamore Community is one of a few small experiments trying to find new patterns of Christian life together, living in the secular structure, serving it and speaking to it.

The Sycamore Community, at State College, Pennsylvania, does not live communally but it shares with the other groups the notion that only small disciplined bands of believers can make Christianity relevant. The "secular city syndrome," it says, is essentially meaningless, for what is needed is bold, even scientific experimentation in living. One test-tube Sycamore chose is American sexual mores, based on its understanding of Christian concern for the needy, the underprivileged. As one of Sycamore's founders, Rustum Roy, a naturalized American from India, a well-known physical chemist and a professor at Penn State, once told a group of Negro Black Power leaders, "You've got an exaggerated idea of being oppressed and persecuted. There is greater oppression in many parts of the world and even in the U.S. today. The most oppressed person is not the Negro but the single woman."

In searching for "new ways of Christian life together" the Sycamore group decided that a morality which ignored the physical and emotional needs of a large body of the population was wrong and unChristian. Single men could do as they liked, but single women were still bound by the rules, even though, in the U.S.A., there are 10,000,000 more women than men. The result was the unwilling spinster, toward whom the Christian community ought to be exercising concern, which might be friendship and caring, but which might take a sexual form as well. The person who might be in the best position to minister, in this sense, to the single woman was the married man.

"We said, 'Okay, what's the problem?'" Roy says. "The original guidelines had failed and nobody was producing new ones. We had no stakes in the *status quo*, so we tried to look at things objectively and come up with new guidelines. We spent years in investigating the issue, and we sent out questionnaires to concerned Christians and talked to people aware of the realities of life. No woman, according to legend, would accept another woman in her husband's life, but the questionnaires and conversations showed that this was untrue. They would do so, as Christians. We don't mean to make sex a palliative—the problem for the single woman may be that she needs friends. We're not advocating kicks. But insofar as friendship risks sex, even with a married woman, it's worth it if it helps change the unhealthy possessive pattern of present man-woman relationships. We feel that if a woman has had a relationship with a married man, and it goes bad, at least she's had something. All relationships should be conducted openly, with the concurrence of all concerned parties. From our limited experience we've found that such relationships work best when the women live in different towns. Wives, of course, should be free to have relationships with unmarried men or widowers. When human need is present, relationships out of marriage may be the vehicle of faithfulness to God. We think that since the churches are partly to blame for current sexual attitudes they should be also responsible for changing them."[1]

Dissenters like Roy play a role in national church groups but they display no interest in conventional parish religion, and, indeed, it's unlikely that the parishes could tolerate their unorthodoxy. Consider the experience of a well-known theologian named Clarence Jordan. In 1942, Jordan came to south Georgia, where he had grown up, to begin near Americus, in the heart of the old plantation "black belt," an experiment called Koinonia Farm. Koinonia, the concept of Christian fellowship and sharing, was to be Jordan's response to the war. Approving neither of fighting nor of his ministerial draft exemption—Jordan did not want to be a chaplain but he offered to serve in a non-combatant capacity and was refused—at least, he thought, he could grow food. And he would open his doors to all as an expression of fellowship and, ultimately, relevance.

Jordan, a former superintendent of missions for a Baptist association, started Koinonia with $65. Within a decade the "collective" owned the 1,100-acre farm outright and as many as a thousand guests passed through there every year, staying weeks or months, with a dozen families living on the farm full-time. Everything was free, and while Jordan was plainly pleased when the resident population worked the farm, there were no rules and no one was compelled to do anything.

On the question of Negroes Jordan was careful not to antagonize the local whites, at least not overly. Negroes came to Koinonia for study and social activities, but none actually lived there. In 1950, though, an Indian agriculturalist arrived at Koinonia. The farm used the most modern horticultural methods in the area and some of its crops, like sweet potatoes and cotton, were also grown

---

[1] For a full treatment of the Sycamore Community's theology and sociology, see Rustum and Della Roy, *Honest Sex* (New York: The New American Library, Inc., 1968).

in India. The visitor was interested in Christianity as a possible religion for his own people and Jordan took him to the Baptist church. "The Indian was shunned," Jordan recalls. "Southern Georgia wouldn't shake his hand. He decided that Christianity wasn't for India, which already has a caste problem. I was humiliated."

Jordan dates his freedom from local customs from this incident, which made him despair of gradualism. Promptly he opened his doors to Negro families. He drove their children to school because, for Negroes, there was no school bus. Though Jordan was a nationally known Baptist preacher, the result of these activities was his expulsion from the local Baptist church, which also meant that he and his family were out of the denomination since membership in a congregation is the key Baptist affiliation. (After that, at church conventions, Jordan would put on a name badge saying "Ex-Baptist," and curious ladies, peering at it, would sometimes say, "Now *there's* a branch of our church I've never heard of.") He went to the other local churches asking to be a member and was turned down by them all.

The situation simmered but in 1954 when White Citizens Councils were organized in reaction to the Supreme Court's desegregation decision, the harassment began in earnest. First there was a boycott. Local merchants wouldn't sell Koinonia food, gasoline, or even fertilizer. The tactic having failed to dissuade him, Jordan was next pursued in the courts. At Koinonia there was a summer camp for underprivileged children, and Jordan was charged with corrupting the morals of minors, who, it was said, could see pigs mating. Unable to pursuade any local lawyer to represent him, Jordan, a plainspoken but humorously eloquent man, defended himself. He replied that he had been unable to teach pigs modesty and the case was dismissed. Other charges followed—evading local taxes, being a Communist—Jordan does not remember how many accusations were made against him.

Although Koinonia was a profitable farm, boycotts and trials were expensive and for a six-year period the farm lost between five and ten thousand dollars a year. When neither losses nor legal harassment dislodged him, his opponents turned to violence. Night after night the cars roared down the road, pausing in front of the farm, guns booming. "It was a miracle," Jordan says, pointing to bullet holes in the walls of the frame farmhouse, "that no one was hurt." Koinonia operated a roadside stand which sold vegetables and country hams. After it was dynamited Jordan abandoned it. The farm fences were cut and the Koinonians had to mount a round-the-clock vigil to keep the cattle off the roads. One day ninety carloads of armed Ku Klux Klansmen drew up in front of the house, offering a compromise. They would buy the farm, they said, if Jordan would leave. His answer was predictable, and the firing began once more.

Jordan was brought before a Grand Jury on the charge that his story of being attacked by armed men was a lie, calculated to foment disorder. "The only way we could prove ourselves not guilty was to get killed," Jordan says. A chain-store owner, passing through Americus and hearing of Jordan's ordeal, ordered his local branch to break the boycott and sell supplies to Koinonia. The store was blown up, but the dynamiters used too much powder and they blasted as well the bank and the courthouse. Even for Americus, it was too much, and the two years of violence finally stopped.

Jordan's communal Christian experiment had been underway despite boycotts and bombing. It was a success but not an unqualified one. The farm had developed a thriving mail-order business in fruits and nuts, but even so there were always problems with money. Many of those arriving on the farm, for instance, needed expensive medical and dental treatment, having been uncared for in the past. "We provided everything," Jordan says, "and it created dependency, a sort of welfare set-up, with the many leaning on the few. Of course we never ordered anybody to work, but there were, I'm sorry to say, some malingerers." Koinonia still took new arrivals, but it began to ask that they be able to care for themselves financially, and once the outside pressure was off, the community gradually broke up.

Jordan was thinking of picking up and trying again in another place. "I'd hoped," he told a visitor one day, "that we could re-establish contact with the larger community, but alas, it is not to be. Here it is 1967 and we still have to drive sixty-five miles to cash a check. Perhaps it's time to leave. People here might find change easier if they didn't feel they had to save face. Myself, I haven't changed. I still believe in the humanity of God, that love works no evil, though I don't know if I can call myself a Christian; if I am one I know I couldn't be a church member at the same time—there are too many tensions. Now that it's all over, of course, the Baptists might want to reclaim me. Maybe I could be the ex-Baptist of the year!"

The religious search for justification through relevance has met many obstacles—indeed, it may be easier for a camel to pass through the eye of a needle than for churches to enter the world. Not least among the difficulties is the resistance demonstrated by the church population, and, in despair, the relevance-minded religionists increasingly abandon organized religion, driven toward what are to them larger ends. For the churches the complete loss of the activists would be a heavy blow, meaning a sharp decline in churchly energy, already declining. But there might still be hope for relevance, and for the disaffected to remain in the religious bodies, if the larger church population could be made to abandon traditional beliefs and attitudes in favor of a new receptivity and openness. The problem is what to do with God.

Chapter Nine

Why God Died

How I wish that God were back
In this world cold and wide
For though some virtues he did lack
He had his pleasant side
              —DON MARQUIS

A HEAVENLY detective, investigating the demise of God on earth, would be obliged to note several odd circumstances.

Item One: The ideas expressed by the cemetery theology of the death of God are not essentially novel. They have been explored by philosophers for at least the past hundred years, by Friedrich Nietzsche, for instance, or Alfred North Whitehead who wrote in 1926, "The modern world has lost God and is seeking him." Though the Death-of-God squad, or "minitheologians," as they've been called, modernized their subject, it hardly took theologians by storm.

Item Two: God's death was featured everywhere, including *The New York Times* and the cover of *Time*. (Peculiarly enough, it was ignored by *Casket and Sunnyside*, the magazine for morticians.) Why should old theology be front-page news?

It seems likely that millions of people never received God's earlier death notices, or were reluctant to heed them. They had to be ready to accept the shock. It follows that whatever the virtues of Death-of-God theology, its larger significance must be sought in the American religious environment.

"Three fairly young men write books," says a knowledgeable churchman, Prof. Daniel Williams of the Union Theological Seminary, referring to the Death-of-God trinity, Thomas J. J. Altizer, William Hamilton and Paul M. Van Buren. "None does first-rate work. They're bright but none has proved himself as a scholar. Yet they've upset the whole theological applecart. What does it mean? I'm inclined to take it seriously. They wouldn't have gotten this kind of attention without touching something vital. A kind of theological self-confidence has collapsed. It may indicate that Protestants can no longer cope with the modern world."

Traditional formulations of the deity, postulate the Death-of-God theologians, are passé and meaningless. Whether they are "true" or not is somewhat beside the point, for what matters is that modern man feels that they are devoid of significance and he experiences a sense of loss, of hollowness, of being abandoned by the traditional deity. "The heavens are empty!" Altizer, spreading his arms, announced to a large congregation, while according to Hamilton, the theologian of today doesn't really "believe in God, whatever that means, or that there is a God, or that God *exists*." Van Buren prefers not to be identified with the Death-of-God movement but, although his work has to do with linguistic analyses of religious statements and beliefs, he too argues that God-talk is a "dated way" of relating the faith to the world. "Christianity," he asserts, "is about man, not God."

One way to approach God-Is-Dead theology is to compare it with attacks on the gold standard. For just as gold believers think that, without gold, there would be no stable basis for currency, so God-believers think that without the God-standard there would be no stable basis for anything, nor, for God-hoarders, would church-liness be freely convertible in heaven. Going off the God-standard would cause panic among those who put their faith in the Ft. Knox God, seeing Him as the guarantor of permanence, the un-derwriter of established rules, values, and theological systems. "Theological self-liquidation," said Norman Vincent Peale about Death-of-God theology; for Reinhold Niebuhr, God's death would deprive the faith of a "rational order." The man-standard, as proposed in the Death of God platform, was seen as not suffi-ciently stable, subject to the fluctuations of human temperament, and in the end too optimistic in its assumptions of human capac-ity.

If the churchly big guns reacted so did the ministers, who pep-pered Death-of-God theology with thousands of sermons. When the man on the street believed in God's death—albeit a watered-down version of what His gravediggers had been attempting to say—then what motive would he have for getting up on Sunday morning to hear the pastor preach? It was feared that God's death would make nuns widows and throw ministers out of jobs.

Despite what they said in public, many ministers discovered that God's death crystallized their own doubts. "Quite a few," reports Rev. Ruell Howe, director of the Institute for Pastoral Studies, which counsels clergymen, "come here as a last resort wondering if they should get out of the ministry. Part of it is due to natural frustrations but these are accelerated by writings on the obsolence of the church and the death of God."

At first look, the Death-of-God theology indeed appears to be an assault on organized religion itself, challenging its principal doctrines and encouraging doubt and wavering among its servants. "If Christ is present wherever there is full human energy or life then it would seem to be apparent that He is more fully present outside rather than within institutional bodies," Altizer believes, and, for Hamilton, the movement into the world appears to mean separation from the church, at least to some degree. " 'Death-of-God theology' assumes," says a writer in *Commonweal*, "that commitment to the world cannot co-exist with a commitment to the transcendent Lordship of God in Christ, and that genuine secularity is an impossible posture for a Christian who continues to take seriously the reality of the Church as the Body of Christ." So, on the face of it, the theology of the Death of God is a fifth column aiming to subvert organized Christianity.

Earnest churchmen may also have feared that the subversion was going to be successful. Church-going Americans, 95 per cent believers in God, received His *momento mori* without apparent tears. They may have even rejoiced at the Bad News, on the sly. "The death of God was a chance for the middle class to follow its desires and cop out of organized religion altogether," thinks one knowledgeable minister. After all, in millions of minds, churches stood for probity, denial, hard work (at the expense of leisure), personal sacrifice, a prissy attitude toward sex. If you could shake God you could shake the churches; you could be rid of the queasy feeling that the tiresome minister, after all, was right because he spoke with divine authority; you could take the pleasure-plunge, free of guilt, hell-bent for hedonism. It doesn't appear to be an accident that the leading purveyor of God-Is-Dead theology for popular audiences is *Playboy*.[1]

For traditionalist, organizationally minded churchmen this dreadful package—containing the Death of God, secularism, hedonism, and atheism—contained a time bomb for religion and ought to be immersed in cold water as rapidly as possible. As Bishop Ladislow Rubin told the Synod of Bishops in Rome in 1967, ". . . some tendencies of contemporary theology—the theology of secularization or the Death of God, present above all among a group of North American Protestant theologians—have affinities with the exclusive interest in the 'terrestrial city' which

---

[1] An orthodox Freudian could easily interpret the Death of God as an attempt to kill the father. This God-father would be perceived as a repressive figure emphasizing tradition at the expense of freedom, rules at the expense of pleasure. Killing the father would be a symbolic means of liberation in order to achieve personal maturity and selfhood.

clearly inspires contemporary atheism . . . the terrible evil of our epoch." If God's dead, in this view, so is the authority of the church, and therefore His continued existence must be acclaimed by the churches. "God Is Alive" claimed a series of Protestant radio ads, and Billy Graham even offered proof. "I know that God is alive," he announced, "because I talked with Him this morning."

Under such lights the Death-of-God theology is clearly regarded as religiously negative, to be fought and conquered. But it can also be argued that God's death is an institutional imperative for the churches, so that the so-called cemetery theologians are bent on redeeming organized religion, just as traditional religionists are destroying it. For if God-Is-Dead confirmed the secret doubts of many, it also offered the possibility of religion without God. It explained to the churches what was happening around them and if conventional belief was irrelevant, radical belief might be relevant indeed. "The first axiom of an authentically contemporary theology," Altizer has written, "is the acceptance of the Death of God." The accent was still on theology; the belief was still *religious* belief. The Death-of-God theologians were, and remained, churchmen; through their affiliation with the church structures they tacitly affirmed the churches themselves.

It's worth noting that Paul Van Buren was once a contemporary Calvinist, a follower of the German theologian Karl Barth, who took the strict view that religion must be separated from culture, in a dogmatic style. Then a teacher at a seminary, Van Buren went to factories in Detroit, where he explained to the workers his high-flown Christianity. "They looked aghast," testifies a minister who was with Van Buren. "They understood nothing and cared less." The minister is convinced that Van Buren's conversion to the Death of God was at least partly the result of the theologian's despair that pure Christianity could ever be explained to the people. "Van Buren," he says, "then set out to analyze what in the faith could be made meaningful, and it did not include God."

The point is made explicit in the thinking of a lesser-known but powerful God-Is-Dead theologian, Rabbi Richard L. Rubenstein. God died for Rubenstein at Auschwitz, for if God existed he was in history, and he thereby bore responsibility for the concentration camps. Such horror simply could not be equated with the existence of God. Bury religion? Not at all. "I do believe in the God of nature," the rabbi says, "the cannibal deity, the old pagan vision of the world, man as a part of nature. I define religion as the way we share the decisive moments of life with our community, our collective participation in the universal rhythms, expressed through rituals. And these will be found in churches and synagogues."

For these theologians church doctrine must be stripped down, simplified, made universal, and unlike more traditional religious thinkers they are able to live in a universe of chance, without the old stable God-standard. But this is to prepare religion for the future and provide a religious home for the increasing numbers whose faith is shaken or gone. God died to save the churches. Did he die in vain?

Chapter Ten

The Future

THE Creator may judge things differently, but by virtually any standard known on earth—the trends in membership, the morale of its junior officers, the clergy, the certainty of its purpose and sureness of its grasp, the respect attached to its pronouncements, or the vitality of its ideas—organized religion in America is in trouble. The condition is well known to churchly chief executives even as they plot population trends, try to figure the right places to buy land for still more churches (while worrying about how to fill the ones they have), and talk bravely about mission in the seventies and eighties. What Rabbi Abraham Joshua Heschel says about the Jews might easily be applied to any denomination or creed: "Our existence as a people is like a mountain suspended by a hair."

The question of just how serious the trouble is necessarily involves the future—the structural, functional, and ideological shape of churches to come—which means in turn the larger society. It may be an index of the importance of churches in the not-so-faraway future that out of many dozens of contributors to the report of the Commission on the Year 2000,[1] only one took up religion in a serious manner, and his conclusions were not notably optimistic. Among churchmen the mood varies, from those who think that religion will have to make few accommodations to society to those who talk about closing the churches, firing the clergy, selling the properties, and giving the money to the poor.

The Pope may warn about "insidious dangers" facing the churches, but it's not really thought by many that American parish religion will wither and disappear in the immediate future. Some people will go on joining churches, marrying and baptizing their children there, putting on their finery on Sundays and driving to worship. There will be bazaars and cake sales, choirs and acolytes, the bespectacled, grimly cheerful clergyman and his yoke-fellow-in-Christ. In short, there will be church as usual, now and seemingly forever, amen.

The trouble with this picture—from the churches' point of view —is that it reveals nothing about size, quality, power, and influence. For the speculation is that the ranks of Christian (and Jewish) soldiers will constantly thin—relatively in terms of society and absolutely in terms of their own numbers—until very few and mostly old people will bother with church at all. The trend toward smaller churches would be greatly accelerated if the outside society decided to tax the religious structures on the grounds that they are private clubs, meeting private needs, for church members would then be required to pay for their religion in full, a commitment

[1] American Academy of Arts and Sciences, Commission on the Year 2000. See *Daedalus*, Vol. 96, No. 3 (Summer, 1967).

few church leaders think the average parishioner is up to. Now churches are, whatever else they are, organizations, and no organization man, ecclesiastical or otherwise, can look with equanimity at the prospect of decline. Besides, the churches still claim to have moral and ethical insights and authority, and not only must they demonstrate that assurance to the outside world but they must placate an ever larger, noisier, and more dissatisfied minority within church walls which feels that religion is not doing its prophetic job. Coming from within and without, then, is enormous pressure on the churches to change. (Indeed, in striking respects organized religion resembles a patient in psychoanalysis, seeking to resolve deep-rooted problems, which means, for churches on the couch, finding more effective ways to act.)

One of the basic models for churchly change is ecumenicism. As conceived by a principal apostle, Eugene Carson Blake, now executive secretary of the World Council of Churches, the proposed Protestant merger envisions a "universally accepted ministry and sacraments, a single standard of membership, and a central planning and administrative authority competent to assume responsibility, in behalf of the now-united ministers and members, for all their significant corporate activity from that point on." Churches at this stage would still retain "residual identity" and authority in various areas but their major undertakings would be under a single council and, eventually, the various doctrinal differences would be hammered out, over a period that might take twenty-five years or more. The Consultation on Church Union, or COCU, is moving in this direction and some day, it's hoped, the Catholics will be brought into the fold. Indeed, as some Protestants conceive it, the United Church in the U.S. would be Catholic at its core, and be organized into dioceses, each with its bishop, diocesan priests and so on.

Such schemes appeal to many churchmen because unity would end the (to them) deplorable differences over essentially unimportant matters of doctrine and organization and permit churches to speak with one hopefully powerful voice; and unity would also solve the problem of the little local churches which are expensive to operate and aggravate the shortage of ministers. But, although ecumenicism may look good on the drawing board, it has some very formidable hurdles before it.

For one, the ecumenical urge is not really governed, as John Wright, Roman Catholic Bishop of the Diocese of Pittsburgh puts it, "by positive religious affirmation, but rather by the fear of what will happen if we don't get together." The fear, of course, is the constant sapping of church strength, and while Bishop Wright believes that fear has often been a better motivator than love, it must also, in the case of churches, contend with still other fears of what will happen if ecumenicism works.

It could mean, in the name of efficiency, the closing of many denominational institutions, like schools and hospitals which overlap in function or serve only the organizational needs of particular denominations. It could portend great defections from those who identify with the separate personality of their church and its doctrines. Two sociologists report, ". . . our data indicate that the fissures which map what might well be called the 'New Denominationalism' fragment the very core of Christian perspective. The new cleavages are not over such matters as how to worship God properly, but whether or not there is a God of the sort that it makes any sense to worship; not over whether the bread and wine of communion become the actual body and blood of Christ through transubstantiation, or are only symbolic, but over whether or not Jesus was merely a man. These disagreements . . . exist substantially *within* the formal boundaries of the Christian churches. In the light of these findings it seems difficult to account for the hopes and activities directed toward general ecumenicism."[2]

If conservative groups are not likely to go along with ecumenicism—"We want no part of it. We'd have to give up too much," says a Southern Baptist spokesman—many liberal churchmen

[2] Charles Y. Glock and Rodney Stark, *Religion and Society in Tension* (Chicago: Rand McNally, 1965), pp. 117-18.

take a dim view of it too. For such critics ecumenicism is an institutional façade covering up the almost total lack of commitment on the local level, a dangerous psychological device for letting church life continue in a self-centered and self-satisfied groove. Ecumenicism, in this view, is nothing more than "pushing the furniture together."

There are variations on the unity theme, like city-wide churches —the Church of Chicago, for instance—which would have ministers from all denominations. But all ecumenical proposals seem likely to run head on into the ethnic and class clubbishness of American churches on the one hand and, on the other, the notion that after all was said and done ecumenically the churches would still be tottering. "Even if the most exalted dream of total Christian union could be achieved," says a leading Catholic lay intellectual, Daniel Callahan, "there is no longer any certainty that it would have a decisive influence on the future of the world."

Such reasons have often led church reformers to work within the framework of their own religious organizations where, in any case, they see plenty to do. Take the Institute for Freedom in the Catholic Church, which includes leading Catholic intellectuals from coast to coast. The church, they hold, ought to be organized not as at present on monarchical but democratic principles, with the popular election of bishops and participation by lay people in decisions. There should be optional celibacy, the phasing out of parochial schools, a de-emphasis of churches as the only places in which to worship, and an end to the ban on birth control. "I'm a believer in institutions—man can't be man without them," says Eugene Fontinel, chairman of the department of philosophy at Queens College in New York City, head of the Institute; "but no institution as such is indispensable. Institutions must be changed toward the realization of the values and visions of a community. Our criticism of the Roman Catholic Church is that its great visions and ideals have been frozen in institutional forms which once served the Church but do so no longer. We hope to see a willingness to restructure—to get rid of some features and to transform others. Our criteria is the quality of life, in and out of the religious community.

"What's happened, in a rough way, is that the Church turned its back on the revolutions that were shaking the world. Emphasizing authority and certainty, the Church has intensified its rigidity for the last four hundred years. It achieved its very identity by being against revolution and change. So Catholics themselves were identified by certitude, by all believing the same things, by having no doubts that the Catholic Church was the true church. These ideas persisted in the face of dramatic historical changes, but during World War II, at last, Catholics had extensive contact with non-Catholics and their rigidity and exclusiveness began to collapse, along with the simplistic Catholic anti-world idea. The 1950's saw a more sympathetic attitude among Catholics toward modern notions, culminating in Vatican II which was really a catching up. For better or worse, it brought the call to Catholics to take seriously the call of other men. Catholics, feeling it was a time to act, got excited, decided the current institutions were not adequate and—but here is the crisis! For Pope Paul, though admitting the institution could be modified, at the same time said not in any fundamental sense. The hierarchy wants it both ways, going along with ideas of change but not really changing. We don't think this is workable. If Roman Catholicism cannot be separated from its present forms the Church is finished."

Gazing starrily off into the future, reformist Catholics see a church which, if it had a Pope at all, would have a non-Italian one. His powers would be greatly reduced and gone would be the spirit of what Philip Scharper calls "triumphalism." The papal tiara would be seen as an inadequate symbol for a church dedicated to serving the poor and overcrowded. The clergy—men and women—would be married or, says Monsignor Ivan Illich, "An adult layman, ordained to the ministry, will preside over the 'normal' Christian community of the future. The ministry will be an exercise of leisure rather than a job. The 'diaconia' will supplant the parish as the fundamental institution in the Church. The periodic meeting of friends will replace the Sunday assembly of strangers." The "great white whale" church architecture would be replaced, too, by geodesic domes, tents or halls rented jointly by various church groups, their old churches having been torn down for housing projects erected with church money.

Just how hard such innovations would be to put into practice is illustrated by the resistance of the faithful to such comparatively small things as the modernization of sisters' habits. "If we change," remarks Sister Charles Borromeo, bitterly, "especially visibly, the entire collection of Catholic images, often fixated in grade school, collapses. Can eternity really exist if sisters change their clothes?" Recognizing the strongly traditionalistic streak in the religious population, some churchly seers anticipate a kind of mixed model, with small, modernistic sects—like The People, in Washington, D.C., which celebrates an "action mass" with bannered processions and cacophanous instruments in friendly parishes or high school auditoriums—managing to exist within the conventional larger church; there would be perhaps dual membership, in a parish and a small group, presumably satisfying everyone. Everyone, that is, except the bishops, who are wary of sapping the already weakening parishes and creating dozens of churchly anti-parties and the dread possibility of schisms, from too much "enthusiasm."

No one, for all the talk, really knows what a Catholic Church as envisioned by the reformers would look like, but there are those who suspect it would strongly resemble the Protestant churches now. And even with freedom and democracy, the Protestants have troubles enough of their own. One of the great unanswered questions facing organized religion—reflected by empty churches and deeply dissatisfied preachers—is what are churches supposed to *do* in modern society? What justifies their existence and keeps them going? What roles are they supposed to play? Some believe that churches ought to be neighborhood centers, changing from WASP-nests to open communities, welcoming everyone. The sociologist Talcott Parsons believes there's a place for ministers as "spiritual counselors," not as part of the present "sanction system" but as sorts of psychoanalysts of human values. Norman O. Brown, the author of *Love's Body*, would transform religion's "priceless insights into a system of practical therapy, something like psychoanalysts" to make them useful and meaningful.

One wonders if the idea of being quietly useful will really satisfy the crusading minister who feels himself "unavoidably summoned," as Harvey Cox puts it, to change the world. For the churches want more than a narrowly utilitarian role. Only the prophetic role, for many servants of the churches, has any real allure. And, since the secular siren is irresistible, the prophetic function must be directed toward social issues to matters of practical policy like Vietnam and civil rights. Christianity, according to the gospel of Cox, ought to be "promissory" like Judaism, promising for the earthly future rather than trying to reveal eternal truths.

If religion doesn't go in this direction, churchmen fear, it risks becoming invisible. "We must reach out to people or we lose credibility," says R. H. Edwin Espy, General Secretary of the National Council of Churches. But by becoming so socially minded the churches risk the defection of the conservatives and a watering down of the faith to the point where it is barely distinguishable from that of the liberal wing of the Democratic Party. I asked Dr. Espy what was, in his view, the irreducible minimum of the Christian religion. It is, he said, "the transcendental view of God and the centrality of Christ. If religion merges with culture to the point where it loses the old idea of God, who is absolute, then we are in real trouble."

From this point of view, at least, the churches may be in real trouble already. One of the catchwords in contemporary Protestantism is that religion must aid man to "becoming human" or even "truly human," whatever that means, and the "model" is Christ. Take the "obvious things" about Christ as listed by a contemporary minister:

He was a popular and controversial preacher.
He gathered a group of followers.
He spent most of his time with the disinherited.
He taught with authority.
He never married.
He never (as far as we know) held a job.
He did not participate responsibly in public affairs.
He did not have income, property, or a fixed address.
He was in bitter and frequent conflict with the religious and political authorities.
He seemed to expect the world would be imminently, radically and supernaturally transformed.
He attacked the traditions and values of his own people.
He practically forced the authorities to prosecute and execute him.[3]

There is nothing exclusively religious, much less Christian, in this description, which with a few exceptions might apply also to Socrates or Che Guevara. I asked many socially oriented ministers why they were Christians at all. Some said through faith, and some said that Christianity gave them courage and the motivation to endure (but so do other beliefs). Some said they hardly knew, and if another more acceptable ideology came along they would embrace it.

The noticeable drift in modern religion away from traditional structures and belief has brought with it problems not just in identity but in maintaining the institutional church. Catholics may well wonder, as they abandon symbol after symbol, why they call themselves by that name, and Protestants why they belong to a church at all. Indeed, warns Paul Ramsey, the Protestant theologian, the church is becoming a "secular sect" and the desire to tell the secular world how to handle its troubles is "a fig leaf to cover the unseemly parts of a disintegrated Christian understanding."

For critics like Ramsey, who puts himself in the category of a conservative dissenter, the churches ought to retreat. They should be heard, to be sure, but from the vantage point of a serious religious understanding and a solid base, which means giving up

[3] Scott Paradise, *Journals*, mss. Journal 20, November 12, 1964 to January 20, 1965, pp. 1-2.

the American concept of denominations and returning to sects, to much smaller bodies of believers who educate their young in church schools financed by themselves, who carry the religious torch and pass it along in this "sub-pagan" culture of ours. The great body of bad believers who populate the churches should be ushered out. Only by stricter, more disciplined and ethical religious life can anyone remain a Protestant, a Catholic or a Jew. Only in this way will anyone "remember the Lord's song."

To other equally earnest Christians the trouble with the sect idea is that a major reform would quickly empty the churches of those they have left. "This might be all to the good," writes Daniel Callahan. "Christianity of the church variety has been mainly a fraudulent, useless business anyway (to talk sect talk). But if you empty the churches, then of course you won't have many people left whom you can change, educate and gradually bring around to a better version of Christianity; and there would be a loss in that. Anyone who has talked with sensitive priests and ministers knows how many of them struggle with this dilemma. If they don't tell their congregations the full, hard, undiluted truth, they feel they will be selling out. But if they do tell the whole truth, they feel they may lose along the way many who might in time be brought to the whole truth."

Change! the churches are always being told, in the manner of Margaret Mead, the anthropologist, who insists they must "be shaken loose from their imprisonment within the archaic forms of a vanishing society." But the options, it seems, always cancel out whether they be an ecumenical church or sects, secularism or pietism, prophecy or tradition, chance or stasis. The evidence thus suggests that serious, far-reaching change will be exceptionally difficult for organized religion in America, and it appears likely that churches will be forced to try to go on in much their present shape. Gradually, as seems politic, they will relax some of their outdated rules, and gently they will try to remove their neat distinction between the spiritual and the material, putting the emphasis on the community rather than the inner life. Religion will probably become more secularized, humanistic, perhaps even atheistic—"poetry plus rather than science minus," as one prognosticator put it—but it will try to retain its identity; that is, it will stay churchy, down deep, and somehow untransformed.

The balancing act such a stance requires will put the churchly bureaucrats to the severest test. Consider the inevitable Catholic confrontation with birth control. The pill may have been hard to swallow, but immediately having ingested it, the church must confront still other devices like the "morning-after" pill, which churchly logic clearly will be forced either to prove is not an abortion device or give way in its rules on abortion. There is no way of resolving such issues without alienating large numbers on both sides. The battles will be numerous and costly between liberals dissatisfied with the speed of change and conservatives who want no change at all. Indeed, some prophesy a schism in the churches between conservatives and liberals, and while a real split seems unlikely the battles will grow and the defections increase, especially among liberals. One of the agonies of modern religion is that a great many dedicated, highly motivated individuals feel trapped, imprisoned, emasculated within its walls.

Defections plus increasing public apathy toward organized religion equal dwindling churches, and the day will almost certainly come, if it hasn't dawned already, when Protestants and Catholics will recognize themselves in the position of Jews, as small minorities in an indifferent, even hostile culture. This will not be a pleasant experience for people accustomed to being the majority, imposing their will and getting their way, but it is written on the wall, just the same. But even if smaller churches are precisely what some reformers advocate, there is no guarantee that they would be different in spirit or that they could hold their own. Indeed, the experience of Jews is instructive, for the Jews, increasingly religionless, intermarrying at a high rate and dispersing throughout the U.S., may themselves be melting into the secular majority.

"There is no sound basis on which to build after demolition," said the Protestant theologian Dietrich Bonhoeffer, a believer in "religionless Christianity," and he is echoed by many of today's religious leaders and principal thinkers. "The Christians will form only a relatively small minority. . . . Christians will be the little flock of the gospel . . . perhaps continuing to bear witness to the holy message of their Lord only in an undertone, from heart to heart," says the Catholic theologian Karl Rahner. "The churches are in a tremendous state of flux," says Dr. Espy. "If I put a high priority on organizations I'd be pessimistic. The American parishioner must understand that the church before many years will not be like the church today. It's not impossible that the church will have to go underground." "We get an inkling of what is to happen by looking at Christian communities in Communist countries," says Episcopal Bishop Daniel Corrigan, "—no money, no jobs, no status, no right to propagate our ideas, but an exalted attitude toward Christianity." "We're headed for a long, cold winter," says Roman Catholic Bishop John Wright, for whom winter means spring, the time of rebirth. But there is no sign in the heavens that organized religion in America will be granted a resurrection.

Chapter Eleven

Sermon from a Secularist

"One of the most effective defense systems against
God's incursions has hitherto been organized religion.
The various churches have provided a refuge for fugitives from God—His voice drowned in the chanting,
His smell lost in the incense, His purposes obscured
and confused in creeds, dogmas, dissertations and other
priestly pronunciamentos. In vast cathedrals, as in little
conventicles, or just wrapped in Quaker silence, one
could get away from God." —MALCOLM MUGGERIDGE

SAVANTS and seers may cry from the mountaintops that our times
are post-Christian and post-religious, but the news has hardly become part of that curious bundle of customs, traditions and myths
known as the American way. If this is the morning-after ideology,
America has a sizable religious hangover.

"As societies become secularized," says Harvey Cox, "the
orientations they produced and nurtured often continue to function long after the symbolic grounding of the orientation has lost
its credibility." If Western man once found satisfying explanations
of reality in religion, he looks now to science or scientific method

to frame the questions. For wonder, he looks to art or outer space, and for reverence, if he has any, he looks to man. Nonetheless, though having outlived their value for many people, religious attitudes and expectations persist. A classic claim of organized religion is that it serves as a kind of storehouse for the idealistic, humane, and moral in American culture, constantly replenishing the short public supply. Indeed, since religion would take credit for some of the "good" in the American personality it seems fair to ask whether the religious contributions to shaping the American mind might have had some unfortunate results as well.

For many Americans religion still serves as an ego-crutch, a way of claiming personal, racial, even national superiority. Exclusivity, self-righteousness, a narrow competitiveness (as revealed in the use of church statistics), financial retentiveness, a desire to impose one's will on others as a kind of enforced brotherhood—such attitudes are all too characteristic of American parish life. Generosity, tolerance, compassion, a willingness to accept ambiguities and take risks—such qualities of mind and heart often appear alien to today's organized religion.

Some churchmen, concurring in this indictment, go on quickly to say that what you see in American parishes is not religion at all but a grotesque cultural distortion of the real thing. "God," they say, quoting Dietrich Bonhoeffer, "has granted American Christianity no reformation." But why has the "real thing" failed to emerge? Is there a flaw in religious—at least organized—religious thinking itself?

For the secular observer one characteristic that stands out as specifically and identifiably religious is "an unquenchable ontological thirst," as Mircea Eliade calls it. (This urge appears even among those who have left conventional religion behind, perhaps as a religious residue.) It consists of a longing, from vague and wishful to strong and demanding, that there be some purposeful intelligence somewhere, some unifying explanation, some overarching rationality and reason for things. Religion in its soul wants ultimate answers, and it wants to stamp meaning and order on the universe, according to its own terms. Ideas that might seem natural to a truly secular mentality—alienation, an essential formlessness about things, the conviction that meaning simply stops when words (or symbols) can no longer describe, the feeling that life does not require absolute answers, the belief that people can act in the best interests of themselves and others without a supernatural goad, an irreverent, humorous, hopeful, serious, chance-taking, systemless, demystified, open-eyed, love for life, ones own and other's—are to the religious man rather strange, even menacing, ideas to be fought and conquered. It may be that this religious "quest for certainty" as John Dewey called it is not unrelated to the American effort to impose its WASPish will and authority on the world, to its inability to tolerate (in the name of order) situations in which the outcome is unknown, even though we justify our actions with talk of the "national interest."

If organized religion wants to be relevant the way is not to abandon its theology and ideals, as it seems sometimes all too willing to do. Indeed, religion appears to act like a person whose low self-esteem will make him do almost anything to be popular. But instead of trying to blend with secular culture, religion could separate out, declaring itself distinct from secular man and his thinking.

Those churches which are obsessed by relevance to the point where there is little or nothing distinctively religious left might well stop calling themselves churches and give themselves another name or disband altogether, since it is quite apparent that much of their ministry and membership do not believe in the official formulations of faith or anything approaching them. At any rate, a ruthless honesty would add to churchly credibility. As a first and necessary step the churches should call quits to the fantastic assertions—obtained only by careless and self-interested counting, and by the inclusion of the vast group which is religiously indifferent—that they speak for the majority when in fact they are no longer sure who they can call their own. The minority status of religion ought to be reflected in the statistics and standards of church membership and shouted from the pulpits. The churches should deny, categorically, that we are "a religious people whose institutions presuppose a Divine Being." If organized religion wants to help clear our aching, fuddled, post-religious heads it would no longer support the vague sentimental genuflections paid religion by political candidates; it would not participate in claims that the country's churchy goodness gives it a certain superiority; it would not offer prayers at affairs having nothing to do with religion; it would steer clear of talk about our "Judeo-Christian heritage" and even help define what our secular heritage is.

Although such proposals do not seem radical they contain certain implications many church people would be unwilling to accept. For if organized religion accepts the primacy of secular man it must also accept his claims. These revolve around freedom, self-determination, self-responsibility, and self-definition. In short, they mean that man must decide for himself in matters affecting his own life. The churches should abandon their opposition to liberalizing or ending the restrictive laws governing divorce, birth control, abortion, adoption, sexual morality, and the like. On such matters they should speak to their own, without attempting to compel the compliance of others. As it is, operating as efficient minorities, churches and church groups do thwart liberalization and cause years of bitter slugging in the courts—needless battles because the churches will eventually lose.

Nor should the churches try to decide how much restriction secular society will place on its members. And if secular America feels there should be a body to deliberate standards and hold up shortcomings, let it form its own—a department of Morality, Ethics, and Wisdom (MEW) with cabinet rank. The churches should refuse to let secular society shrug off its responsibilities on them.

Another claim secular society would make on the churches is to subject them to taxation, a critical step in the disestablishment of American religion. For honest religion would try to support itself, without depending on the largesse of the outside world. The tax exemptions and many kinds of state aid offered the churches not only keep them alive but institutionalize them within secular society. Although the state, with its post-Protestant hangover, doubtless sees religion as an instrument of stability, there is really no evidence that the church contributes greatly to social gain or that its prayers for society have brought results. If this is the case, state-supported religion is unfair to everybody—to secular man, who pays for it, and to the churches which decisively compromise themselves.

A secular state which taxed religious property on the grounds that it is owned by a private organization serving its own ends would not be expected, obviously, to finance church schools. Just as the parochial school system appears destined to die in the United States, so taxed churches would be considerably smaller. But most important, the real separation of church and secular state envisioned here would mean forthright recognition on both sides that the divorce is permanent, that just as the state will refrain from using the churches for its own purposes so the churches will eschew "subsidiarity" or any long-range ideas of reunification.

Here, though, one might offer a compromise. Just as the churches would be expected to refrain from coercing secular society, so the state should not coerce the churches. "The power to tax is the power to destroy," said a Supreme Court decision, and the right of the state to tax the churches might also mean state power to regulate or undermine religious organizations. For this reason, and because volunteer organizations should be kept alive, the state should not tax that part of the churches used for services, that is, the sanctuaries.

To say that the religious population is a minority in the United States—a statement religious leaders themselves confirm—doesn't mean that this minority isn't sizable, true to its convictions, and devoted to its faith. Many people, and not merely the old, the sick, the lonely, and the neurotic, find solace in the churches, and while a more active, out-looking credo than parish religion provides might sometimes bring a happier, more purposeful existence, there is no reason to doubt that supportive religion is necessary for a considerable group. (These are what William James called the "tender-minded" as opposed to "tough-minded.") In the churches, too, are a great many dedicated, motivated, active people who have demonstrated, time and again, their commitment to the welfare of others. Nor can the ideals of religion simply be written off. As Walter Kaufmann has said, ". . . if we are made to choose between reason and religion, the choice is between criticism and idolatry. Whatever in religion cannot stand up to criticism is not worth having—and this means a great deal, but it does not mean everything. Among the things that remain is the aspiration which is the soul of religion."

Many qualities are missing in the life of secular man—feelings of awe, privacy, poetry, depth—but as a non-believer he will not find them in organized religion. Secular man will have to look deeper into his soul, toward the kind of secular idealism fashioned by Harold Laski: "The quality that is of the essence of a religion is the inner and passionate impulse which drives those who possess it beyond and above themselves to an elevation where they can conquer the immediate desire, and the temporary caprice, in their search for a fraternal relation with all who suffer and all who are broken by the tragedy of the pain they cannot face. . . . This religion existed long before any of the historic religions were born, and it will live on long after many of them are dead. It has no institutions, no dogmas, no rituals, no priests; it is a spirit. . . ."[1]

With this spirit, organized religion will have to compete. In the end, says Leslie Dewart in *The Future of Belief*, Christianity has a "*mission, not a message*. . . . What it communicates is its reality and existence, not an idea." To communicate its reality, its aspirations, the churches must know themselves and their members.

[1] Harold J. Laski, *Faith, Reason and Civilization* (New York: The Viking Press, 1944), p. 320.

Whether religion is considered tradition or revelation, the churches will be forced to show that they bear witness to a meaningful faith, as demonstrated by their own actions and lives. There is always the smallest chance that the churches—in some fashion yet undefined—are right, but the proof is up to them.

Index

179

Bearings for Re-Establishment, 68, 82
Bell, Daniel, 17
Benedict, Don, 140
Benedictines, 80
Berger, Peter, 93–94
Berne, Eric, 94
Bible, The (film), 17
Bier, Father William C., 77
Billings Hospital of University of Chicago, 97
Birnbaum, Norman, 18
Birth control, 7, 9, 16, 120, 163, 169, 174
Bishops' Commission on Pastoral Counseling, 76
Black power, 143, 148
Blake, Eugene Carson, 118, 161
Blanshard, Paul, *American Freedom and Catholic Power*, 31
Blizzard, Samuel, 60 and *n.*
"Blue chip" Protestant denominations, 33–34
See also Congregationalists, Episcopalians, Presbyterians, and Elmhurst, Illinois
B'nai B'rith, 108
Bonhoeffer, Dietrich, 4, 44, 170, 172
Booth, Gotthard, "The Psychological Examination of Candidates for the Ministry," 84–85, 85 *n.*
Borromeo, Sister Charles, 70, 165
Boston Industrial Mission, 141
Bowers, Margareta, *Conflicts of the Clergy*, 74 *n.*, 87–88, 87 *n.*
Boyd, Malcolm, 12
Are You Running with Me, Jesus?, 136
Brande, Lee, "The Rabbi: Some Notes on Identity Clash," 65–66 and *n.*
Breeden, James P., 142
Brown, Norman O., *Love's Body*, 166
Buddhists, 23, 26

California Migrant Ministry, 139
Callahan, Daniel, 163, 168
Calvinists, 89, 157
Campbell, Ernest Q., and Thomas F. Pettigrew, *Christians in Racial Crisis—A Study of Little Rock's Ministry*, 61–62 and *n.*, 97 *n.*
Camus, Albert, 133

CARE, 125
Carmines, Al, 136
Carthusians, 76
Casket and Sunnyside, 154
Catholic Psychological Review, The, 80 *n.*
Catholic Relief Service, 125, 126
Catholics, Roman, 10, 21, 22, 24, 40, 58, 86, 103, 105, 108, 109, 115 *n.*, 117, 119, 121, 122, 124, 127, 128, 138, 144–45, 161, 163–65, 167, 169
and corporal punishment, 73, 83
and defection of priests, 10–13, 54, 66–73
and mental illness in priests, 76–84
opposition to psychoanalysis, 77, 80
poverty claim of, 128
and public relations, 5
and race question, 19–20
statistics on, 6, 7, 26, 28–30
Celibacy, 67, 69, 71, 72, 77 and *n.*, 84, 163
Center for the Study of Democratic Institutions, 12
Center of Intercultural Documentation, 68
Chardin, Teilhard de, 100
Charity, 129–30
Chesapeake Foundation, 140
Chicago Theological Seminary, 50, 132
Register, 39
Christadelphians, 26
Christensen, C. W., "The Occurrence of Mental Illness in the Ministry," 90 *n.*
Christian Advocate, 60 *n.*
Christian Century, The, 60 *n.*, 147
Christian Scientists, 25
Church of Chicago, 163
Church of Christ, United, 25, 34, 49, 103, 109, 111, 136, 138
Church of the Covenant (Elmhurst, Ill.), 50
Church of Daniel's Band, 26
Church of Jesus Christ (Cutlerites—Latter Day Saints), 26
Church of the Savior, 145–46
Church World Service, 125, 129
Civil rights, 47, 61–62, 95–96, 104, 127, 144, 166